T0316563

# Y Tu Mamá También

Charting production, distribution, censorship, and reception, this book examines *Y Tu Mamá También* in its presentation as a journey of self-discoveries. Three young adults enjoy a road trip together in search of a legendary beach. Behind their stories are *mythologies of youth*, a network of ideas in the film that reflects life outside the theaters. The deceptively complex film leaves the characters and its viewers with, instead of oversimplified and hollow answers, provocative questions and existential concerns. Made independently in Mexico, the film crosses over transnational issues, global markets, and mainstream and alternative aesthetics. It transforms road movie and youth film genres and shows a 'musical, magical' Mexico to the world. This book synthesizes several approaches in order to extensively examine *Y Tu Mamá También*. Covering the film's production history, its distribution and censorship, and larger industrial, political, and cultural contexts, this book analyzes the too-often overlooked aspects of youthful sexuality alongside figurations of maturity, rites of passage, and covenants—made, broken, and remade—that not only inform representations of identity but also complicate the processes of identity formation themselves.

**Scott L. Baugh** is Associate Professor of English and Coordinator for Film & Media Studies at Texas Tech University. He specializes in Latina/o, Latin American, and multicultural cinemas. Recent publications include *Latino American Cinema* (2012) and *Born of Resistance* (2015, with Víctor A. Sorell).

**Cinema and Youth Cultures**
Series Editors: Siân Lincoln & Yannis Tzioumakis

Cinema and Youth Cultures engages with well-known youth films from American cinema as well as the cinemas of other countries. Using a variety of methodological and critical approaches, the series volumes provide informed accounts of how young people have been represented in film, while also exploring the ways in which young people engage with films made for and about them. In doing this, the Cinema and Youth Cultures series contributes to important and long standing debates about youth cultures, how these are mobilized and articulated in influential film texts, and the impact that these texts have had on popular culture at large.

**The Hunger Games**
*Catherine Driscoll and Alexandra Heatwole*

**L'Auberge Espagnole**
*Ben McCann*

**The Virgin Suicides**
*Justin Wyatt*

**The Breakfast Club**
*Elissa H. Nelson*

**The Freshman**
*Christina G. Petersen*

**Y Tu Mamá También**
*Scott L. Baugh*

For more information about this series, please visit: www.routledge.com/ Cinema-and-Youth-Cultures/book-series/CYC

# Y Tu Mamá También
## Mythologies of Youth

## Scott L. Baugh

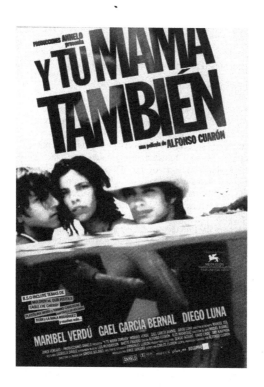

Taylor & Francis Group

LONDON AND NEW YORK

First published 2020 by Routledge

2 Park Square, Milton Park, Abingdon, Oxon OX14 4RN
605 Third Avenue, New York, NY 10017

*Routledge is an imprint of the Taylor & Francis Group, an informa business*

First issued in paperback 2021

Publisher's Note

The publisher has gone to great lengths to ensure the quality of this reprint
but points out that some imperfections in the original copies may be apparent.

*Library of Congress Cataloging-in-Publication Data*
Names: Baugh, Scott L., author.
Title: Y tu mamá también : mythologies of youth / Scott L. Baugh.
Description: London ; New York : Routledge, 2020. | Series: Cinema
   and youth cultures | Includes bibliographical references and index. |
   Summary: "Charting production, distribution, censorship, and reception,
   this book examines Y Tu Mamá También in its presentation as a journey of
   self-discoveries. Three young adults enjoy a road trip together in search of a
   legendary beach. Behind their stories are mythologies of youth, a network of
   ideas in the film that reflects life outside the theaters. The deceptively complex
   film leaves the characters and its viewers with, instead of oversimplified
   and hollow answers, provocative questions and existential concerns. Made
   independently in Mexico, the film crosses-over transnational issues, global
   markets, and mainstream and alternative aesthetics. It transforms road movie
   and youth film genres and shows a 'musical, magical' Mexico to the world.
   This book synthesizes several approaches in order to extensively examine
   Y Tu Mamá También. Covering the film's production history, its distribution
   and censorship, and larger industrial, political, and cultural contexts, this book
   analyzes the too-often overlooked aspects of youthful sexuality alongside
   figurations of maturity, rites of passage, and covenants—made, broken, and
   remade—that not only inform representations of identity but also complicate
   the processes of identity formation themselves"—Provided by publisher.
Identifiers: LCCN 2019024204 (print) | LCCN 2019024205 (ebook) |
   ISBN 9781138079823 (hardback) | ISBN 9781315114248 (ebook)
Subjects: LCSH: Y tu mamá también (Motion picture) | Coming-of-age films—
   History and criticism.
Classification: LCC PN1997.Y24 B38 2020 (print) | LCC PN1997.Y24
   (ebook) | DDC 791.43/72—dc23
LC record available at https://lccn.loc.gov/2019024204
LC ebook record available at https://lccn.loc.gov/2019024205

ISBN: 978-1-138-07982-3 (hbk)
ISBN: 978-1-03-217739-7 (pbk)
DOI: 10.4324/9781315114248

Typeset in Times New Roman
by Apex CoVantage, LLC

# Contents

# Series Editors' Introduction

Despite the high visibility of youth films in the global media marketplace, especially since the 1980s when Conglomerate Hollywood realized that such films were not only strong box office performers but also the starting point for ancillary sales in other media markets as well as for franchise building, academic studies that focused specifically on such films were slow to materialize. Arguably the most important factor behind academia's reluctance to engage with youth films was a (then) widespread perception within the Film and Media Studies communities that such films held little cultural value and significance, and therefore were not worthy of serious scholarly research and examination. Just like the young subjects they represented, whose interests and cultural practices have been routinely deemed transitional and transitory, so were the films that represented them perceived as fleeting and easily digestible, destined to be forgotten quickly, as soon as the next youth film arrived on cinema screens a week later.

Under these circumstances, and despite a small number of pioneering studies in the 1980s and early 1990s, the field of 'youth film studies' did not really start blossoming and attracting significant scholarly attention until the 2000s and in combination with similar developments in cognate areas such as 'girl studies.' However, because of the paucity of material in the previous decades, the majority of these new studies in the 2000s focused primarily on charting the field and therefore steered clear of long, in-depth examinations of youth films or was exemplified by edited collections that chose particular films to highlight certain issues to the detriment of others. In other words, despite providing often wonderfully rich accounts of youth cultures as these have been captured by key films, these studies could not possibly dedicate sufficient space to engage with more than just a few key aspects of youth films.

In more recent (post-2010) years a number of academic studies started delimiting their focus and therefore providing more space for in-depth examinations of key types of youth films, such as slasher films and biker films, or examining youth films in particular historical periods. From that point on, it was a matter of time for the first publications that focused exclusively on key youth films from a number of perspectives to appear (*Mamma Mia! The Movie*, *Twilight*, and *Dirty Dancing* are among the first films to receive this treatment). Conceived primarily as edited collections, these studies provided a multifaceted analysis of these films, focusing on such issues as the politics of representing youth, the stylistic and narrative choices that characterize these films and the extent to which they are representative of a youth cinema, the ways these films address their audiences, the ways youth audiences engage with these films, the films' industrial location, and other relevant issues.

It is within this increasingly maturing and expanding academic environment that the **Cinema and Youth Cultures** volumes arrive, aiming to consolidate existing knowledge, provide new perspectives, apply innovative methodological approaches, offer sustained and in-depth analyses of key films, and therefore become the 'go to' resource for students and scholars interested in theoretically informed, authoritative accounts of youth cultures in film. As editors, we have tried to be as inclusive as possible in our selection of key examples of youth films by commissioning volumes on films that span the history of cinema, including the silent film era; that portray contemporary youth cultures as well as ones associated with particular historical periods; that represent examples of mainstream and independent cinema; that originate in American cinema and the cinemas of other nations; that attracted significant critical attention and commercial success during their initial release and that were 'rediscovered' after an unpromising initial critical reception. Together these volumes are going to advance youth film studies while also being able to offer extremely detailed examinations of films that are now considered significant contributions to cinema and our cultural life more broadly.

We hope readers will enjoy the series.

Siân Lincoln & Yannis Tzioumakis
Cinema and Youth Cultures Series Editors

# Acknowledgements

Greatest thanks go to Yannis Tzioumakis and Siân Lincoln for the invitation to contribute to the CYC series, for impeccable editorial direction and guidance, and—beyond words of thanks—for remarkable consideration and kindness as colleagues. Great gratitude extends to Routledge, especially Felisa Salvago Keys for commissioning the book and Suzanne Richardson, Natalie Foster, Eleanor Catchpole Simmons, Jennifer Vennall, and Richa Kohli for seeing this book through production and to completion. Conversations with many colleagues, media artists, friends, and students are the backgrounds-*becoming*-foregrounds around this project, too many to list but all much appreciated. Portions were completed during a Summer Residency Fellowship at the National Humanities Center, for which exceptional support and generative collegiality I wish to thank the entire NHC and Summer 2018 Fellows, particularly Robert D. Newman, Lynn Miller, Brooke Andrade, Tania Munz, Brian McFadden (Texas Tech University), Esther Fernández (Rice University), Héctor Jaimes (North Carolina State University), Jaime Ahlberg (University of Florida), and more. Generous support came from Texas Tech University, particularly through W. Brent Lindquist's and Brian Still's leadership. I give *mil gracias* to Kent Wilkinson (Texas Tech University) and Jesús Torres (Instituto Tecnológico y de Estudios Superiores de Monterrey) for their generosity and extraordinary collegiality. Ranging conference sessions informed aspects of this work, notably with Michelle Johnson Vela (Texas A&M University-Kingsville), Marco Iñiguez Alba, Erin Claire (Arkansas Tech University), and more. Many thanks to all and everyone I inadvertently have overlooked. Last big thanks I send to my family, Tammy, Washington, and Hamilton, to whom I dedicate all of my best efforts.

# Figures

# 1   Aspirations

Immediately following signature silent white-letter-on-black opening credits, *Y Tu Mamá También* (Cuarón 2001) begins with viewers peering from a hallway vantage through a teenager's bedroom doorway to find her and her boyfriend in a tangle of naked limbs [see Figure 1.1]. Intrigued, do we transport ourselves from the moment and transiently envision our own early sexual educations? Are we vicarious parental figures furtively surveilling or peers peeping in on this young consensual lovemaking? Presented so early in the film, the first-time viewer no doubt will be alerted to empathic, expressivistic, and exploitative possibilities of the sexual representations. Some viewers might pause in dismay or avert their attention, but many will be compelled to discover more. The opening shot triggers a range of questions and experiential responses quite effectively.

Even as the sensual spectacle demands attention, this imagery as a story introduction is like the proverbial groping in the dark. At fade in, precisely half of the frame from right is filled by the darkened wall outside the bedroom. Copulatory bodies appear fragmented in abstract motion. The sexual discourse performs sleight of hand. If half of the scene seems revealed, more than half is hidden. This threshold moment formally (as opening establishing shot in long take) and thematically (as hallway and door passageway) proves as prophetic as it is disarming.

The R-rated version of this film entirely foregoes the initial 24 seconds of this 122-second long take, which is telling in its own way.[1] For viewers of the original not-rated version particularly though, this opening shot offers paradoxical suggestions of inclusion and exclusion, of invitation and boundary crossing, of intimacy and distance, of enticement and observation, of advocacy and scrutiny, of fantasy and graphic reality—in between objectivity and subjectivity—all as a constellation of unanswered questions and only partial or sometimes contradictory revelations. As the uncensored shot plays on, longer than feature-film opening shots normally do, before

*Figure 1.1* Mysteries Around the Corner

resequencing conventional continuity patterns, viewers may find themselves even more in an interrogative, contemplative, searching frame of mind. Indeed, only partial answers cohabit with one another throughout this film.

If the core impulse of *Tu Mamá* is asking questions, particularly the kind of questions that inform forging identity like those most of us ask during the inherently transitional adolescent passage into adulthood or in anticipation of equally significant, complicated, uncertain life changes, then the corresponding core concept of the film enacts a rebuttal against singular, unequivocal, facile determinations. One thing for sure, *Tu Mamá* is deceptively complex.

This exchange of questions and answers appears most clearly and directly in the film's characters, their in-formation maturity and sexual identities, their existential growth and frustrations, and their desire for liberation from fundamentalism; on the way, it also helps justify competing notions of (trans)national political principles, economic philosophies, and several global-cultural issues that surround the characters, their stories, and the film as a whole. Much of this can be situated for viewers in a mix from playful innocence, immaturity, and naiveté to hard-fought, ruminative lessons, first on the individual level but then also collectively as a generation turning to the 21st century. It formulates but never fully resolves a millennial worldview.

Where clearer answers might have offered some stabler (if reductive or even hollow) senses of being, acts of questioning correlate with acts of becoming and progressive, transformative possibilities. Processes of identification systematically override any singular identity or issue as product. Universal, existential associations lift up to metaphysical and ecstatic-spiritual revelations at key moments in the film viewing as profoundly as art experiences can. These are admittedly high stakes for global-commercial entertainment. Youthful sexuality with its painstaking measures of intimacy and vulnerability provides something like a Rosetta Stone, perhaps something between prism and oracle, seemingly miraculous, for the development of these discoveries.

*Y Tu Mamá También* presents a mythological journey of self-discoveries. It depicts three young adults taking a road trip together. Two typically immature late teens, Julio (Gael García Bernal) and Tenoch (Diego Luna), eager for sex, drugs, and rambunctious adventure, fatefully find themselves traveling with an attractive, disillusioned late-20-something woman, Luisa (Maribel Verdú). Tenoch and Julio have finished high school, see a prescribed adulthood looming before them, but linger in the liminal threshold of the seeming simplicity of their adolescence. Luisa learns both of the continued infidelity and sexual indiscretions of her husband, Tenoch's older cousin, and also of a chronic condition that not only explains her infertility but, even more horrifically, will soon take her young life. All three contemplate in-formation and in-crisis identities.

As much as the vibrancy of youthful life does, death travels with the characters. Death correlates with existence, the dread of the former making the latter that much more vital. There are materialist matters involved in the existentialist questions, but, rather than remain static, existence is perpetually dynamic. The film's director, Alfonso Cuarón, deliberates on this point:

> You can't really enjoy life until you have an awareness of death. We tend to have an awareness of death only when something critical happens like the passing on of a loved one. We should have an awareness of death every day. . . . Finding your identity is a life-long, ongoing process, and the more you are aware of death, the more your identity evolves.
>
> (quoted in Lawrenson 2002: 19)

The film does not easily translate the life-death concepts around a simple oppositionality. Nor does it synthesize them into practical social contracts and direct moral lessons. Instead, the film provides enough clues to Luisa's illness that viewers, immersed in the film's questions and mythic explorations, interpretively infer that something is dreadfully wrong but not necessarily the grave extent until disclosure at the story's conclusion. In adolescent cluelessness and solipsism at an extreme, neither Julio nor Tenoch initially detects, nor cares enough to investigate, that anything is significantly wrong.

If things seem half-hidden at start, their journey progressively reveals parts of the story that not only are frequently ignored but prove most difficult to confront. Each character must find some compromise but not full resolve by film's end, and so might we as viewers.

The three travel by station wagon (nicknamed Betsabé, Spanish-inflected Bathsheba) in search of a legendary beach cove known as Boca del Cielo, 'Heaven's Mouth,' intonating simultaneously bawdy and supernal suggestions. The tone of this film veers in and out of sophomoric silliness as much as its teen-driven wagon meanders through country lanes and dirt-road byways, all of which disguise several of its probing messages. As our characters face cruxes, the film reveals comparable changes for the end-of-century Mexican nation and the world. *Tu Mamá* frames this Mexican cinema passageway and crosses the threshold into an age of globalization—in art, culture, and commerce. Interrogations of Alfonso Cuarón's auteur branding, collaborations with his brother Carlos Cuarón and cinematographer Emmanuel 'Chivo' Lubezki, and *Tu Mamá*'s aesthetic give shape to this passage.

The filmmakers aim in *Tu Mamá* to devote equal weight to characters and to the contexts and environments that surround them and us, according to Alfonso Cuarón, 'one to inform the other or clash with the other' (quoted in Galloway 2014). Through readings of this film, viewers will come to appreciate that *clashes* are no simple thing. Frequently presented thematically as disputed facts, half-truths, and outright lies, contradictions, unrealized promises, or even paradoxical positions, a strange dialectics leaves viewers less fully informed and more puzzled, arguably, than genre-heavy mainstream commercial cinema does by rule. Rather than merely representing current issues, *Tu Mamá* exposes several of the social structures and institutional models behind these issues and displaces their values. It equally exposes its own narration and artistic convention and, in a poststructuralist method, re-sequences them in an address to its viewers.

If global-commercial cinema by the end of the 20th century theoretically conflates activities of expression and reception-perception according to prescriptive codes (representational, narratological, generic, etc.), then reimagining the discursive relationships among filmmaker, spectator, and film, as Vivian Sobchack contends, returns the 'film experience' to an 'originary activity of cinematic signification' (1992: 9–17). Before differentiating structural codes restrain heuristics, a film and its viewer both contain and make sense: an 'address' between them operates according to phenomenological modes of sensuous 'becoming' that yield 'wild' meanings, 'primordial' considerations of in-formation existence (*ibid*: 17, 11). Upon 'radical reflection,' retrospection that (re)constitutes experiences, Sobchack argues, 'embodied' realities appear mediated but also radically materialized; imaginary but also historically and cultural contextualized; synthesized through regulatory structures but then also thoroughly 'undone' (2004: 1–4, 1992:

6–9, 89–93)'. The 'proof' is not when a viewer actually lives any single experience but when an 'experience's structure [is] sufficiently comprehensible' that a viewer 'might "possibly" inhabit it (even in a differently inflected or valued way)' (Sobchack 1992: 5).

*Tu Mamá* advances a film experience that partially satisfies the tendency toward classical paradigm readings and cultural codes but then also highlights opportunities to redress them. It teases viewers with provocative, sensuous themes that prompt radical reflections on structured experiences—some stereotypical, some ceremonialized—to expose and destabilize the structures (artistic and social) and the values concording them. Disarmingly, *Tu Mamá* denies any individualistic-heroic stance, dramatizing adolescent immaturity and identity crises but emphatically overcoming them through assemblages of intra-, inter-, and extra-subjective perspectives and characters-in-place experiences, multiply contradictory identifications simultaneously. Backgrounds resituate foregrounds, actions repeat, and storylines and aural-visual details counterpoise against one another.

The experience certainly replicates those around the approach to adulthood—cycling through adolescent indecision and uncertainty, venturing toward the unexpected to see what comes from it, hoping but frequently failing to be entirely original. *Tu Mamá* advances a *youthful address* that does not as much precisely depict adolescence as it interrogates processes of becoming that are inherently exploratory and transformative, that remain ever-potentially revolutionary but insoluble, and so can be overwhelming and debilitating. The stylistic exigencies of *Tu Mamá* bring attention to exemplary stories of adolescence that mimic early-21st-century experiences, especially for a transnational-globalized Mexico, but also elevate beyond allegory.

*Tu Mamá* presents stories as *mythologies of youth*. Roland Barthes's *Mythologies* (2012) collects not classic 'mythologies' one might expect but rather everyday dramas. Notoriously, professional wrestling, celebrity weddings, royal odysseys, generational advertisements, astrology ethics, striptease art, movie iconography—all serve textual analyses for patterns around 'high' and 'low' expressions; spectacle; conventionality; and ceremony, ritual, and tropes. Not any one mythology tells the whole story: significance lies in the networks they trace. Mythologies play a 'constant game of hide-and-seek between the meaning and the form,' like a recognizable symbol that is 'indisputable' but also 'has too much presence' (*ibid.*: 227–8). The contextual presence is:

> tamed, put at a distance, made almost transparent; it recedes a little, it becomes the accomplice of a concept which comes to it fully armed . . . once made use of, it becomes artificial.
>
> (*ibid.*)

Myth in this sense 'hides nothing' yet 'flaunts nothing': it compromises a 'third way' between the two that generates 'distortion' and 'deformation' toward reinvented meanings; its form paradoxically calls out then dismisses in 'rapid alternations' of associative meanings (*ibid.*: 240, 232, 227). Considering a poststructuralist cinematic aesthetic sheds light on the full potency of films, described somewhat oxymoronically by Philip Watts as a 'Barthes cinema,' that utilize techniques as part of a '"syncopation of meaning" capable of emancipating viewers' from 'alienating rhythms of attention' (2016: xviii). A third way reconceives the rhythms, which may further open up arrhythmic options.

*Mythologies* proves that audiences make their free-will choices informed by the codes: personal stories depict themes and correlate with allegory and history for collective messages; sometimes personal stories involve growth and existential crises; structures that represent these and offer identification with them also can contain and perpetuate scripts; values seem naturalized and appear largely associational but normalized. Radical reflections upon the meaning-building artificiality expose codification and allow decolonizing processes.

It is interesting, first, that this argument delivers for its death-of-the-author author Barthes what many consider to be a crucial transition in his career between structuralism and poststructuralism (Belsey 2002: 38–43). And as a result of his work among a handful of the most influential theories, scholarship crosses a threshold in approaches to modern textual studies, cultural theory, and related fields. It is more than merely interesting that Carlos Monsiváis's retrospection on Mexican cinema discusses rigidly conceived 'mythologies' that emphasize the role of melodramatic visions of the world as 'the filmic equivalent of maturity' and that national cinema's 'profound reason for being' (1995: 117, 127). His 11-item manifesto-like list of 'mythologies' overviews ways that canonical Mexican films themselves and the industry as a whole provided national endorsements on 'entertainment, family, unity, honour, "permissible" sexuality, the beauty of the landscape and customs, and respect for institutions' (*ibid.*: 117).

Taken as a whole, Monsiváis's set of 'mythologies' explains the preference for configuring these national themes and issues 'within Hollywood-derived cinematic structures' (*ibid.*). Exactly this conversation over 'mythologies' and their structures coincides with transitions in the careers of *Tu Mamá*'s filmmakers and for international and independent art-narrative cinemas crossing over national markets toward global-commercial mainstreams at 21st-century turns. *Tu Mamá*'s aesthetics enact generative responses to structural patterns in cinema and culture, especially through configurations of adolescence.

Mythological youth correlates teen years with the necessarily transitional developments toward adulthood. Independence and self-centeredness weigh against cooperation, intimate relationships, and social responsibilities. We humans explore and create, we invent, and we try to understand and explain ourselves—our very existential being and our aspirations of *becoming different* through the processes of growth. Sexuality plays a keen role in envisioning ourselves as adult-forward, not childlike, but something in between and incomplete. Ceremonies and rituals script some moments. We push against boundaries and find our positions among conformity and nonconformity. With autonomy in sight, we range emotions through ecstatic revelations to depressing gridlocks. Moments stutter. Life repeats itself awkwardly. We loop around and find ourselves back where we started sometimes (or feel that way). Yet we find ways *forward*. As much as we defy typecasting or oversimplifying the complexity, the best stories do too.

*Tu Mamá* conveys mythologies of youth. These stories enact 'ways of reacting to things' and may afford better recognition of those around us and our social conditions. Sometimes the mythologies of youth feel confused, like listening to two different songs at once or like discovering things do not add up. Mathematics, metrics, science, and tradition cannot be trusted fully. Ignored ideas come forefront. The greatest goals—more than clarity in understanding each other absolutely—are discoveries of freedom in intimacy, sexual and otherwise, and empathy for one another, ethically and morally. Spirit exceeds logic. We seek diversion and wildly new experiences. We travel a road that mirages into a river that opens to the sea; inexplicable forces deliver us to a fantastic spot with unfathomable opportunities. For some, the sublime of the sea shows the material impermanence of our lives. Hopes and dreams translate into eschatological concerns. Can true significance be realized in one lifetime? Still, many probably lack the courage to actualize those possibilities in this world, may even avoid asking the questions, and return to the humdrum (sometimes). Virtue arrives through confronting the questions.

This book synthesizes several approaches in order to extensively examine *Y Tu Mamá También* and its mythologies of youth. Chapters 2 and 3 discuss the film's production, its distribution and censorship, and larger industrial, political, and cultural contexts that include philosophical and artistic influences acknowledged by the filmmakers. From Chapter 3 forward, aspects of youthful sexual developments help to decode the film's complex aesthetics—systemically alternating stylistic patterns. Discussions borrow from a number of fields, including language theory, history, cultural anthropology, psychology, even music theory, precisely to advantage the range and significance of the poststructural reinventions in *Tu Mamá's* complex resequences.

With attention to narratological and generic frameworks, Chapters 5 and 7 initiate youth movie considerations that extend through the road movie. Chapters 6 and 8 consider how modern revolutions redefine sexuality as a function of intimacy and identity building, which enacts a kind of gravitation force for neighboring chapter topics and conclusions outlined in Chapter 10. This book takes particular advantage of aural-visual close reading to analyze the too often overlooked aspects of youthful sexuality alongside figurations of maturity and development, rites of passage, and covenants—made, broken, exposed, and remade—that inform not only representations of identity but also the complicated processes of identity formation themselves.

Playful attention to manifestoes as historical documents helps to shape the organizational strategy of the book, highlighted in Chapters 4 and 9, and Chapter 11 ingeminates the film's own epilogue. Yet, ultimate conclusions emphasize how explorations of youthful sexual developments reveal processes of identity formation that transcend itemized lists and manifesto-like articles. The film exposes the artistic and social structures and loosens their dominant-hegemonic attachments to value-laden concepts. As such, *Tu Mamá* and its mythologies of youth enact a hopeful vision and practical realization of revolutionary possibilities at the turn of the 21st century. Better than being left with limited but falsely reassuring answers, viewers are left with provocative, profound, and uplifting questions.

## Note

1. Unless otherwise stated, this book references the 2014 Criterion Collection DVD as the uncensored, not-rated/NR version and the 2002 MGM DVD as the censored, R-rated version. Criterion English-language subtitles compare to actual spoken word and dialogue from the film's soundtrack and the Cuaróns' 2001 Spanish-language screenplay, translated by the author.

# 2 Creativity

The making of *Y Tu Mamá También* repeats the adage: an overnight-success story that took over ten years to realize. Ideas for *Tu Mamá*'s story emerged around the late 1980s (Anhelo 2002). The Cuarón brothers tried several times to draft their story about young people making a trip to the beach, but the 'project never really came together' the way they and cinematographer Chivo Lubezki wanted, and 'it was shelved a long time' (*ibid.*). Notably the three kept stumbling on generic aspects—particularly the superficiality of current mainstream teenpics and linearity of the road movie—and realized they had been restraining themselves according to certain 'preconceptions'; they equally recognized the importance of having the right support to reach the potential of this project (Cuarón and Cuarón 2001: 5–6).

Over this same ten-year period, while *Tu Mamá*'s story would lie in wait, the filmmakers began building what would prove to be enormously successful careers. In film school, attending the Center for Cinematographic Studies (CUEC) at the National Autonomous University (UNAM), they encountered artistic and political disputes with faculty and gained reputations for being self-proclaimed 'arrogant brats'; on the other hand, they also saw themselves banding together around the potential of 'film language' and global markets rather than serving the establishment's 'very ideologized' 'communist' agendas and remaining stranded in domestic markets (quoted in Galloway 2014). Written by Carlos Cuarón, shot by Chivo Lubezki, and co-edited, directed, and produced by Alfonso Cuarón, *Sólo con Tu Pareja* (1991) represents the first major milestone for the collaborative team. Financed by Mexico's Institute of Cinematography (IMCINE), *Sólo* was stunted by what the director called 'paternalistic' state sponsorship (quoted in Fernández 2001).[1] A disgruntled IMCINE held up distribution for almost two years then grudgingly released it to Mexican theatres, where it proved a national hit. From its domestic commercial success and critical recognition, the filmmakers moved to the mainstream (Shaw 2013: 160).

After shooting *Sólo, Like Water for Chocolate* (Arau 1992), and *Miroslava* (Pelayo 1993) in Mexico, Lubezki worked in the U.S. with Ben Stiller on the generational anthem *Reality Bites* (1994) and then again teamed up with his compatriot Alfonso Cuarón on *A Little Princess* (1995) and *Great Expectations* (1998) through Warner Bros. and 20th Century Fox, respectively. The two features employed increasingly larger budgets, bigger stars, larger crews, and demanded a commensurate reliance on studio mechanisms, conventional aesthetics, and mainstream expectations. Cuarón as director and Lubezki as director of photography primarily answered to producers Mark Johnson and Art Linson, respectively, for the two projects. *A Little Princess* won critical attention and has grown into something of a cult classic but was not marketed well and lost on its $17M budget, earning only $10M during its theatrical release, whereas *Great Expectations* won back its $25M budget and received mixed reception.[2] Both are entertaining films in many respects. The director nevertheless reflects back on *Great Expectations* as 'a complete failed film' but a bitter lesson, and Lubezki agrees that it was their 'least satisfying' professional experience (quoted in Lang 2016). By comparison, *A Little Princess* provided a 'good experience' with a studio because the filmmakers found 'no interference' (Cuarón, quoted in Galloway 2014).

In sum, creative control and global ambitions battling against national and international industrial contexts gives contour to the filmmakers' shared journey from the late 1980s to the late 1990s. The filmmakers did not define success merely by profits or critical praise but valued their ability to manage their collaborative efforts within an industrial context. Their work sought progressively larger audiences. And finally, although this story follows some aspects of a traditional auteur model, it better reflects the marketing savvy efforts of building a brand. By the time the *Tu Mamá* project resurfaced, the filmmakers were ready to platform the Cuarón brand of film language.

One major turning point for the making of *Tu Mamá* came when Alfonso Cuarón discussed the project with Ted Hope, co-founder with James Schamus of the New York-based independent production company, Good Machine International (GMI) (Cuarón and Cuarón 2001: 5–6). The same year *Tu Mamá* was initially released, Universal acquired GMI—one more indie-shrinking and rich-getting-richer story in the rise of the 21st-century entertainment industry's conglomerates. Months before that though, Ted Hope went in search for an independent project that could deal smartly with erotic material. This sparked renewed interest in the project, and the brothers revisited the premise and rewrote the script in about three weeks (Pulver 2013). As they tell it, they listened to Frank Zappa's music and talked about *La Nouvelle Vague* films for inspiration, often with Chivo Lubezki's contributions (Cuarón and Cuarón 2001: 6). They also acknowledge that they 'could never convey all the elements' until they had the support of GMI to put 'it in an erotic context' (Anhelo 2002).

An equally important turning point came for the production when the director convinced prominent Mexican businessman Jorge Vergara to produce *Tu Mamá*. Together they co-founded the independent production shingle Anhelo (Spanish for 'yearning').

The Production Notes stress that Vergara as producer 'has always guaranteed Alfonso complete freedom as a director, the best production quality possible, and freedom from interference or censorship' (Anhelo 2002). This reads one-part contractual to two-parts promotional. Perhaps as a playful representation of their working relationship, Vergara's only other important role in the film is acting as Mexico's president in attendance at Tenoch's sister's wedding. Although the hand-held shot seats him center and front, knowingly he faces away from the camera, literally self-effacing the producer. Further suggestive of creativity surpassing executive power, the camera 'stands' over the stilted proceedings of the toast. The image denies any one Mexican president or any singular 'Mexico' in order to interrogate the complicated social condition and its multiply iterated legacies, all mirrored by Anhelo's international financial arrangement and *Tu Mamá*'s cross-over independent production scheme (Cuarón and Cuarón 2001: 6–7, 115 n13). The filmmakers favor a minimalist, 'small production' that itself registers 'intimate' connections among the cast and crew and yields levels of autonomy and collaboration difficult to find in the studio-anchored productions they had just completed in *A Little Princess* and *Great Expectations* (quoted in Galloway 2014).

The filmmakers approached casting for *Tu Mamá* with a combination of interests. Non-professionally trained actors might lend the film's realism an advantage, but Cuarón decided the 'chemistry' among the characters was something 'crucial' that only highly adept actors could provide (Anhelo 2002). More, there were a few method-based creative strategies that the filmmakers devised around the characterizations.

Gael García Bernal and Diego Luna had known each other practically their whole lives. At the time of *Tu Mamá*'s casting, too, they had both worked together as well as competed for parts in Mexican television and stage productions. Both enjoyed lead roles and increasing fame in Mexico on the popular telenovela *El Abuelo y Yo* (1992), Luna was winning more television and stage roles, and García Bernal had a hit with *Amores Perros* (González-Iñárritu 2000) the year before *Tu Mamá*. The director noted that this real-life relationship of collegiality, friendship, and trust but also 'competition and rivalry' among the young men, which they described as a 'common language' not far from that shared among the filmmakers themselves, could inform the 17-year-old characters of Julio and Tenoch (quoted in Basoli 2002: 28).

For *la Madrileña* Luisa, Cuarón chose a Spanish actress who might lend some trans-Atlantic diaspora and feelings of relative alienation against the film's *Mexicanidad (ibid.)*. The director looked to Maribel Verdú, whose career spans fashion modelling and acting on stage, on television, and in dozens of feature films in Spain, most notably as ingénue in *Amantes* (Aranda 1991) and sensuous fiancée in *Belle Epoque* (Trueba 1992). Verdú brings a combination of experience, charisma, international appeal, and an alluring screen persona to her part as Luisa.

The director claims that he limited the actors' interaction and rehearsals leading up to *Tu Mamá*'s first shoots and that the film was shot heavily in sequence, which meant that as the 'ice melts' between the actors and as Verdú grows more comfortable being in Mexico, the characterizations and production could borrow from this 'as a tool' (quoted in Kaufman 2002). Add to this the filmmakers' claim that the cast and crew gained trust like a family taking a trip together and shared collaborative energies, the actors particularly improvising and adapting dialogue (quoted in Basoli 2002: 29).

There are likely very specific aspects of Julio's and Tenoch's late-1990s *Chilango*-Mexico City slang informed by the young actors. Although a few years older than the characters they play, García Bernal asserted for himself and Luna that adolescent experiences and generational connections were 'very much fresh in our minds' (Anhelo 2002). The Cuaróns' screenplay situates original lines that were red-lined and replaced with more current (and oftentimes much dirtier, more vulgar, and richly ambiguous) slang spoken in the film, and it includes a four-page glossary of phrases used in the film to bridge intra-generational and international gaps among the cast and crew (2001: 7, 243–6). Later Cuarón brand films *Children of Men* (2006) and *Gravity* (2013) generate their own small multimedia universes, most directly with the semi-autonomous texts *Possibility of Hope* (2007) and 'Aningaaq' (2013), respectively. If a marketing strategy, or even if only a retailing tactic, Anhelo's distribution of *Tu Mamá*'s screenplay nonetheless offers intertextual evidence for readings and remains indispensable.

In between *Amores Perros* and Guillermo del Toro's *The Devil's Backbone* (2001), *Tu Mamá* represents a momentous shift in Mexican and independent world cinema away from state sponsorship and control while transfiguring current international coproduction models (Smith 2003: 389–400; Shaw 2011: 117–19). With *Tu Mamá*, the filmmakers return to Mexico for a film that fuses national and transnational gestures for global-commercial audiences. Although the director claims to avoid revisiting his films once they are released, both Alfonso and Chivo note *Tu Mamá* as a favorite project because it offered a 'great experience' through 'strong collaboration[s]' made possible by creative control outside of Mexican-state control and mainstream production mechanisms (quoted in Galloway

2014). This story of the production, the method tricks for the actors, even the shooting in sequence all deserve some healthy skepticism, however, simply because marketing strategically merges cross-over business and art in relatively complicated patterns.

Particularly through collaborations with his brother and Lubezki, Alfonso Cuarón fairly complicates the traditional auteur notion of director-as-author. Statements by the filmmakers, perhaps all the more, are insightful to this complicated text. And there are tendencies across the body of work that, first, reflect the industrial location and creative control of the production as discussed previously but also, second, reveal the formation of a significant aesthetic shift initiated by *Tu Mamá*.

The first Cuarón feature, *Sólo con Tu Pareja*, updates the screwball genre but favors *Chilango*-yuppie culture in its depiction of early-1990s Mexico City (Haddu 2005: 79). As a womanizer and advertising executive, our main character-hero Tomas (played by Daniel Giménez Cacho, who also voices *Tu Mamá*'s narrator) draws to the surface gender, sexuality, and heteronormative social issues, as well as figurations of commercialism, but the film's light-hearted comedy buckles under the pressure of the timely and serious issue of AIDS. It also notably favors a regressive, macho heterosexuality in most of its humor without balance of alternative views or a wider scope. Like *Tu Mamá*, *Sólo* opens with two lovers entwined, but this time adult characters appear in focus with some note of sophisticated *suavé*; as important, the camera is already in the room (uncannily like the censored R-rated version of *Tu Mamá*), which suggests more of a character-driven subjectivity and an alliance with them than ingress for exploration.

*Sólo* as a whole mostly conforms to mainstream aesthetics, but one noted stylistic departure offers a smooth-moving, wide view of a sumptuous outdoor wedding banquet and grossly comical set of guests around an anxious, lonely groom. The long take, running slightly over 30 seconds, cranes above the (mock-)sanctified proceedings and diverts attention to the wooded trails nearby. A few continuity cuts later, curious children arrive at Tómas enjoying rambunctious sex with the bride, the classical-style editing glossed by Mozart's *Don Giovanni*. Where *Tu Mamá* astutely convolutes tones and perspectives, *Sólo* merely germinates the concept. Race and ethnicity, too, treated with care in *Tu Mamá*, frequently devolve to stereotype in *Sólo*. Young-urban-professional identity glibly overdetermines the Mexican national character presented in the film, and, crucially, classicism stylistically holds it and comparable values in place.

Both adaptations, *A Little Princess* and *Great Expectations*, generally adhere to the classical paradigm too. Aesthetically, these early films mark what the collaborative filmmakers self-consciously describe as a 'green period' for the Cuarón brand, with the color accenting most directly *A Little*

*Princess* and only slightly more subtly the palettes in *Sólo* and *Great Expectations.* Aspects of their early careers disclose emphasis on 'cultivating an identifiable style,' self-promotional acumen, and marketing strategies more so than necessarily their expressionist tendencies or auteur iconography (Shaw 2013: 172, 181; Udden 2009: 36). For instance, when asked why the color green matters, each filmmaker gave a vague explanation for archetypal and emotional associations with the color (Shaw 2013: 171–2). By the release of *Great Expectations,* Cuarón films were being recognized for lush visuals, baroque style, and an opulent (or even overly cluttered) *mise-en-scène.*

The director also pronounced during the making of *A Little Princess* that he was undergoing a 'spiritual awakening':

> life is showing me things that I've not seen before, that I've been sceptical of before. A couple of years ago, I'd say 'Those things are crazy,' but . . . I don't believe in coincidences anymore. They're hidden messages that are given to you.
>
> (quoted in Kronke 1995)

However, *Princess*'s producer Mark Johnson hedged his bets slightly by describing Cuarón's 'very active spiritual life' as part of his convincing pitch for the director job (*ibid.*). Later, around *Gravity*'s release, Cuarón linked rationalism and faith, arguing that 'spirituality and science can coexist' and together provide opportunities for 'change' like identities being 'reborn,' 'where we have new meanings and new knowledge of ourselves' (quoted in Gray 2014).

Regardless of the motivation, appreciation for spirituality is a key ingredient of the evolving Cuarón brand. Some narrative designs account for spiritual issues that transcend rationalism, and their treatment follows the creative control afforded them. From *Tu Mamá* to especially *Children of Men* and *Gravity*, narratives include abstruse, philosophical-spiritual arguments within their storytelling and story-level messages in ways that earlier films tend toward melodramatic sentimentality. There might be narrative puzzles for viewers to sort through, and yet Cuarón's narrative puzzles never present themselves in as obtrusively fragmented or apparent ways as *Amores Perros* does—or as *Pulp Fiction* (Tarantino 1994), *Memento* (Nolan 2000), and *Timecode* (Figgis 2000) do in indiewood; or as *Run, Lola, Run* (Twyker 1998), *Suzhou River* (Ye 2000), and *Oldboy* (Chan-wook 2003) do for that matter in contemporary international contexts.

Smartly describing Cuarón's creative style as 'auteurism in flux,' Deborah Shaw explains how the filmmaker's global-commercial ambitions follow progressions from director-for-hire in his early work to a 'director producer' in later work, with earned benefits of creative control, whose authorial role emphasizes marketing and self-promotion as much as making movies (2013: 157–9, 170–9). Compare these roles with Walter Benjamin's concept of 'author as producer,' whose technique oscillates dialectically between form and content (1998: 87–8). Rather than placing authorship and a work's industrial location and context vis-à-vis production relations of its time, Benjamin proposes critical assessment of their 'position *within* them' (*ibid.*).

In the early years of our new millennium, Alfonso Cuarón professes distinct views on globalization as 'symptomatic of the times we are living in':

> the world is getting muddled in the interacting of different languages, cultures, countries. It is getting more blurred all the time, the line between independent and mainstream and what is considered foreign and domestic. . . . I think it is great. The diversity just triggers new ideas and new schemes and new formulas.
>
> (quoted in Galloway 2007)

Acknowledging that the danger of this is that national, cultural, and artistic traditions will suffer or may even disappear and that cinema may become more homogenized, he replies 'probably, but': 'at this point, it is a beautiful breath of fresh air and breaking the homogenous aspect of cinema . . . bringing to the mainstream table different tendencies' (quoted in *ibid.*). The filmmaker clarifies that he is 'not defending' globalization per se, but 'in the arts, it is a positive expression of this phenomenon; and at this point, it is the opposite of homogeneity' (quoted in *ibid.*). At the time of *Tu Mamá*'s wide release, Cuarón emphasizes that arts in an age of globalization cannot avoid but instead should carefully attend to national and traditional 'problems,' 'plus the ones that are being imported by modernity' (quoted in Basoli 2002: 26). He continues:

> Saying 'I'm against globalization' or in Mexico saying 'I'm against modernity,' is like saying 'I'm against the law of gravity.'. . . The question now is how to democratize globalization and modernity.
>
> (quoted in *ibid.*: 26–7)

Indeed, how can a film democratize globalization without neglecting its network of national/transnational issues? Perhaps as crucial as anything, *Tu Mamá* advances a radical reinvention of cinema's fictive-narrative aesthetics for global-commercial audiences at the turn of the 21st century. Whereas early Cuarón projects were obsessed with looking 'good' by commercial-mainstream standards, *Tu Mamá* designs 'ugly' moments and exposes the fabrication inherent to all representation and all narratives (quoted in Pulver 2013). The aesthetics are 'about decomposing as opposed to composing the shot'; however, the director describes the composing-decomposing as not a simple binary opposition but a processual 'clash,' which is 'not about breaking the rules, but about not knowing the rules ever existed' (quoted in Kaufman 2002; Galloway 2014). The director relates conversations the filmmaking team had: 'Let's do the film we would have done before going to film school' (quoted in Lang 2016). Comparable to 'address' returning the cinematic experience to 'originary' signifying activities, the clash recalls experiences before they were rule-bound and structurally determined (Sobchack 1992: 17).

In *Tu Mamá* the filmmakers 'strip back the technical aspect' that they admitted previous overreliance on, especially for failures in *Great Expectations* (quoted in Pulver 2013). Having earned a reputation for complicated lighting packages in other projects, Lubezki's cinematography in *Tu Mamá* takes advantage of Zeiss Super Speed lenses to account for natural-light and low-lighting setups, especially to situate foreground with background in depth and allow movements through the frame. The director notes that the use of dollies, elaborately staged setups, and conventional editing that were so fundamental to the aesthetics of several earlier films are transformed in *Tu Mamá* (quoted in Fernández 2001). Additionally, real-life outdoor locations, even for highly choreographed action, feed the film's sense of realistic texture and complex authenticity. According to the Criterion commentary, a steadicam operator was hired for the project, but that technique is never utilized; instead a robust array of moving shots carry the characters and viewers through this narrative.

The director notes anchoring his earlier narratives to a subjective, character-driven viewpoint and the need, through the *Tu Mamá* project, for something 'different': 'something objective, seen from the outside,' a model where 'you learn about the characters through the context' (quoted in Feinstein 2002). Aspects of the camerawork sometimes seem to mirror 'the self-absorbed wanderings of an adolescent's mind, as it stumbles over fragments' of 'unfinished thoughts' (Basoli 2002: 26). But the identifications rarely present anything so straightforward as a single character's perspective or focalization. Even when camera movements coordinate with character movements, they almost entirely deny and frequently counteract the heroic qualities associated traditionally with main characters. And just as the long take occasionally may rack outside-in or pan A-B-A to emulate continuity patterns, it refuses close-up contact with any character. The filmmakers claim to deliberately avoid the close-up precisely because it 'separates a character from its environment': in *Tu Mamá* 'character and environment are equally important,' reversibly 'one is the product of the other' (Cuarón, quoted in Pulver 2013).

Moving and hand-held long-take shots, frequently in subtle oblique, are extraordinary in *Tu Mamá*, not just because their 19.6-second average duration far exceeds the mainstream-commercial standards, as James Udden has demonstrated (2009: 28–9). I argue the long takes must be read in correlation with their sequential functions. That is, the long-take shots alternate in systemic ways throughout the narrative alongside and sometimes catalogued within sequences of nuanced continuity editing.

Furthermore, the soundtrack often disguises its own complexity with dynamic range, shifting or competing points of audition and reference, stark rhythmic-arrhythmic contests, contrapuntal forms, and more. And the voice-over narration offers a hypodiegetic level of information that regularly intervenes in the film's unorthodox balance of objective and subjective narrative comprehension (Lahr-Vivaz 2006: 85–7). As Edward Branigan describes narrative comprehension and 'disparities of knowledge' among characters, narrators, viewers, and even creators, 'knowing' normally (and normatively) arranges as a hierarchy based on amount and potential reliability of knowledge (1992: 66–8). *Tu Mamá* complicates these classical paradigm patterns, exposing their differences, and then resequences them for an alternative aesthetic. Far from reading the long-take shots nor their representational imagery in isolation, viewers must confront the entire sequence of *Tu Mamá*'s aural-visual parameters, the values exposed, and the 'logic' they reformulate. Rather than 'knowing,' virtue derives from confronting unsettling questions.

Refining the Cuarón brand, *Tu Mamá* represents a momentous and critically fascinating node in the maturation of the filmmakers' careers, a return 'to their creative roots' (Cuarón, quoted in Galloway 2014). Yet this film defies 'the usual nationalistic criteria,' and the return refers not to Mexico proper but rather to opportunities for 'experimenting' with 'something different' (Cuarón 2007; Anhelo 2002). In his own manifesto, Alfonso Cuarón guards against *Tu Mamá* 'representing Mexican cinema' and advances it as 'also a part of everything else' (2007). The director advises 'people to start cutting loose from those geographic roots, to begin moving towards a state of freedom, of rootlessness' (*ibid.*).

After *Tu Mamá*, Lubezki earns distinct honor as the first cinematographer ever to win best cinematography Academy Awards three years in a row. With *Gravity* wins, Alfonso Cuarón stands among only nine filmmakers in the history of cinema named best director from the Academy, BAFTA, Director's Guild, and Golden Globes for the same film. *Tu Mamá* has proven commercially profitable, critically recognized, something in between cult classic and generational anthem, and exemplary of the best 21st-century cross-over among independent, national, and worldwide markets.

*Tu Mamá* experienced a unique type of platform release (Shaw 2007: 3–5). In June 2001, it opened in 250 Mexican theatres, distributed by 20th

Century Fox. The film made $2.2M USD in its first week, becoming the top-grossing opening by a Mexican film. These figures are all the more remarkable given that Mexican authorities denied under-18 admissions with a category-C rating. The ratings controversy spurred Anhelo to file a lawsuit against the Mexican government over censorship and likely generated its own fair amount of publicity. By the following year, according to *Screen Daily*, Mexico's rating system expanded to include 'B15' and 'D' categories to account for teenage and adult audiences ('Mexico Finally Revises . . .' 2002). Still, lax theatre practices surely allowed plenty of teens to sneak in to see *Tu Mamá*, perhaps emboldening the where-were-you-when mystique in the experience (Shaw 2013: 180).

Between August 2001 and September 2002, *Tu Mamá* played packed houses and won critical recognition at over a dozen festivals worldwide. Most notably it won a Golden Osella for screenplay, acting awards for García Bernal and Luna, and a Golden Lion nomination at the Venice International Film Festival and the FIPRESCI Prize at the Havana Film Festival. GLAAD Media Awards recognized its success at both mainstream U.S. and international gay festivals, while it won best youth feature at the Zlín Film Festival for Children and Youth. Across motley contexts, most directly the story was gaining attention from larger and more diverse audiences through word-of-mouth on the festival circuit.

By October 2001 the film began winning over art-house audiences, and it was officially released in March 2002 through IFC Films in the U.S. and Canada and through 20th Century Fox in Latin America and Europe. Again, rather than bearing the brunt of an adults-only (NC-17) rating, which Bob Berney, IFC Films' senior vice president for marketing and distribution, associated with a taboo connotation, the film was distributed without rating certification (Caro 2002). Theatrical exhibition denied the age group being represented in the film legitimate access to the film. Paul Dergarabedian, president of Exhibitor Relations, a company that compiles box office figures and strategizes feature-release schedules, noted at the time of its official opening that *Tu Mamá* defied two combined 'standard reasons' that a film might not perform well commercially in mainstream markets: its adults-only and foreign status (quoted in *ibid.*). Instead, it succeeded in commercially and critically crossing over these categories.

The screenplay earned Academy Award and BAFTA nominations, and the soundtrack was nominated for a Grammy. It won Best Foreign Feature at the Independent Spirit Awards and was recognized in that category at the British Independent Film Awards, the Golden Globes, and by dozens of critics' associations, including a Special Silver Goddess by the Mexican Cinema Journalists and being named a top ten film of the decade by the Los Angeles Film Critics Association. Not to be overlooked, MTV-Latin

America recognized it in their movie awards for favorite film, for best insult, and for best song categories and included three entries, with various combinations of characters involved, for best kiss.

All told, *Tu Mamá* played in over 40 countries and grossed over $33.5M theatrically worldwide, about 60% of that in non-U.S. markets and 40% in the U.S. It broke Mexico's existing box office record for a domestic film at the time and remains in the all-time top ten almost two decades later (Tierney 2018: 40). Miniscule compared to Hollywood standards, its reported $5M budget is relatively substantial for contemporary Mexican productions. A relatively large investment was put toward aggressive, guerrilla-style advertising, as described by Ernesto Priego, 'a sharp, cool promotional campaign inspired by British film design, including ads and billboards absolutely everywhere, from bus stops, metro stations and public transportation to every imaginable free space in the already-overcrowded, 20 million-plus city of Mexico' (quoted in Shaw 2013: 180). Later, IFC Films targeted ads to Latino audiences for its wider release (Caro 2002).

Notably, the film was marketed and well-reviewed as 'wildly erotic' (Travers 2002), 'unafraid of sexuality' (Mitchell 2001), 'provocatively and unapologetically sexual' (Turan 2002), *ad nauseum*, but as evident in the film's opening images, sexiness clearly does not tell the whole story. MGM's insistence that Alfonso Cuarón edit the aforementioned R-rated version of the film for home video distribution additionally complicates this whole story. Media-specific censorship in the video industry operates according to moral and political standards that discriminate against international productions and protect the MPAA's and its member studios' relationships with sales outlets and their 'conservative economic clout' (Benson-Allott 2009). *Tu Mamá* is particularly exemplary of this maltreatment directed by mainstream video industries at foreign and sexually explicit films.

Ironically, changes that serve the interests of large transnational corporations from the unrated *Tu Mamá* to its R-rated version undercut precisely the criticism against homogenization and fundamentalism that the film advances. Caetlin Benson-Allott smartly makes this point but applies the premise to a reading of the film's 'queer allegory,' with class the 'determining factor' in the 'sexual narrative' (2009). Instead, I submit, rite-of-passage sex along with public nudity, pranks, rudeness, crudeness, and comparable transgressions of social conventions act like depth finders, plumbing the fathoms beneath the seemingly tranquil surface for emotional, behavioral, and value autonomy as part of *Tu Mamá*'s literal and figurative journey toward self-discovery. As a motif in adolescent mythologies, sexuality enacts physical changes but also echoes identity construction and symbolic existential considerations toward adulthood. Where teenpics generically romanticize and deform the importance of youthful sexuality, and road movies generically direct these as linear developments, *Tu Mamá* treats youthful sexual development with greater honesty and complexity. The censorship then highlights forms of hypocrisy that *Tu Mamá* precisely resists and should be read as such. At the same time, censorship also conceives a variant text with its own truth factors that can be read alongside the uncensored version and related authorial materials.

Sexuality is certainly never gratuitous in this film. Arguably the R-rated and unrated versions feature similar representational qualities of its graphic depictions of male and female nudity, postcoital embraces, even enacted and imagined orgies. Add to this that after the Mexican censorship board initially argued for an 18-over rating based on sexual themes, it changed its complaint to depictions of teen drug use without consequence, and both NR and R-rated versions depict plenty of marijuana and ecstasy use (Durbin 2002). Specifically, in total seven moments from the unrated version of the film, restored as a 2K digital transfer in the 2014 Criterion Collection DVD release, were excised in the MGM-distributed DVD version:

- the first 20 seconds of the opening shot [0:47–1:07]
- the last 23 seconds of this same opening shot [2:26–2:49]
- the 106-second sequence at Julio's girlfriend's house before they leave for the airport [2:49–4:35]
- about 15 seconds across three shots, two removed entirely, from the country club pool scene [21:31–21:57]
- 104 seconds from the long-take of Tenoch's and Luisa's love scene [54:26–56:10]
- a comparable 45 seconds from Julio's and Luisa's love scene [1:05: 23–1:06:08]
- and 80 seconds from the Luisa-Julio-Tenoch *ménage-a-trois* [1:32: 49–1:34:09]

In addition to these roughly 393 seconds of excisions, significant elisions and alterations to the soundtrack recast the second half of the opening shot, the conclusion of the pool scene, and as the radiator overheats on the road.

As Benson-Allott reveals, the subtitling of the MGM R-rated version of the radiator scene flatly misinterprets performed dialogue, where non-Spanish-speaking audiences must infer that Luisa suggests anal stimulation ('*¿culo?*') rather than merely touching 'from behind' (*ibid.*). Language translations are always fraught, but subtitling throughout the R-rated version obscures the genuine content of the film's sexual storylines. And yet, because the sexuality serves multiple purposes, the subtitling operates alongside the dialogue in a number of contexts throughout this film with the most important being the characters' discovery of identity and disclosure of maturity—and lack thereof. Reassessing sexuality as questions of intimate experiences is a necessary ingredient to this understanding of *Tu Mamá*.

There is no small irony to the point that one clear aim of *Tu Mamá*'s film-makers was to show greater honesty and deeper significance in the treatment of sexual experience than mainstream, commercial, generic teenpics generally afford, and this is precisely lost in the censorship of the film. Recall in *Risky Business* (Brickman 1983) the first meeting of teen lovers swept away in magical realism's soft focus and wind machine or the end-of-summer pairings in *American Pie* (Weisz 1999), with virginity lost in fairy-tale innocence and Hallmark card-seeming 'specialness.' And on the opposite end of their own romantic-depersonalized spectrum, in one Joel (Tom Cruise) seems to magically penetrate Lana (Rebecca De Mornay) while keeping his pants up, and, well, the other's title reflects on the virtues of penetrating a 'pie.' And both are accessible for mainstream audiences, although sanctioned for their 'riskiness.' Where mainstream teenpics curiously romanticize, individualize yet depersonalize, but still typically sanitize representations of this very significant idea, *Tu Mamá* treats rite-of-passage sexuality with more direct benefit to questions surrounding identity building and maturation. Deeper honesty reveals itself not in the representations but in exposing their signifying processes.

The film's treatments of sexuality as part of millennial transformations of intimacy imbricate the range of seemingly asexual contexts surrounding this film story and these characters. Their explorations of intimacy reveal the superficiality of their in-formation identities and vulnerabilities to the larger national and global millennial condition to which they belong. Endowed with 'youthful sexiness,' the characters are depicted engaging in a range of sexual acts with one another in various combinations. Sometimes graphically represented, the sexual discourse must be interpreted multiple ways across contexts, which the uncensored film more fully allows. *Tu Mamá*'s treatment of youthful sexuality is not the point of the film, however, just as much as any one theme of national identity, class-based privilege, or patriarchal gender roles is not. Yet the concepts surrounding youthful sexuality, in censored and uncensored versions, best decode the complex narrative design of this film and its complicated relationships with traditional and contemporary social models, which our next chapter will consider vis-à-vis the filmmakers' artistic and philosophical influences.

## Notes

1. For fuller discussions on IMCINE and its 1990s funding initiatives, see Shaw (2013: 167–9) and Tierney (2018: 38–40).
2. Financial information derives from reports at IMDb (Internet Movie Database), Box Office Mojo, BoxOffice Pro, and other sources whenever available.

# 3 Originality

*Y Tu Mamá También* is a remarkably structured film. The narrative can be identified in three acts with an epilogue. Act One borrows most directly from the genre of the 'youth film,' and Acts Two and Three travel with the 'road movie.' The Cuaróns' screenplay even includes many notations that highlight plot-point moments and complex reiterative qualities (2001). Upon initial viewing, *Tu Mamá* seems to favor linearity in both character development and travel action. Advanced even further, linear developments then can be applied to allegorical aspects of their stories. These are viable, even compelling if isolated, interpretations. Put differently, perhaps *Tu Mamá* absorbs mainstream viewer expectations for these linear developments and as a result disguises extensive aspects of the narration in which technique overrides the dramaturgy, reversing the 'normal' patterns without delimiting them. Applications especially of the long-take shot, the patterning within continuity editing, the voice-over narrator, and manipulations of spatio-temporal synchronicity creatively complicate the access points viewers have into this film and provide multifaceted identification with its storyworld. Consequentially, lessons multiply in profundity.

According to *Tu Mamá's* filmmakers, diverse (and fairly recondite) artistic and philosophical sources influence the film's aesthetic. They emphasize two textual models, Jean-Luc Godard's films, especially *Masculine Feminine* (1966), and Frank Zappa's music, especially 'Watermelon in Easter Hay' (Cuarón, quoted in Kaufman 2002; Anhelo 2002). Slavoj Žižek makes significant impressions as well. In common across these ponderous, abstruse, and somewhat perplexing conversations is a generatively reactionary approach to structuralism, and this steers back into discovering and better understanding the aesthetic of *Tu Mamá*.

Put directly, *Tu Mamá* advantages a poststructural approach that appeases global-mainstream tastes. Readings of *Tu Mamá* do not benefit fully from the 'intensified continuity,' the hypermediated 'subjective realism,' or the character-based causal-driven narratives definitively characterizing late-classical or post-classical cinema in leading scholarship (e.g., Bordwell 2006: 118–41; Thanouli 2009: 47, 50). Thomas Elsaesser and Warren Buckland conjecture that contemporary global-mainstream styles beyond the classical paradigm 'cannot be established on the basis of a binary opposition such as spectacle vs narrative, nor . . . any other "either/or" construction of difference' (2002: 61). Fred Pfeil, honing in on style, chronotope, and narration precisely, insightfully indicates that the 'real significance' within contemporary cinema 'lies in complex shifts, shadings, exchanges, and tensions that play upon' 'the structuralist *combinatoire*,' their 'nodes of opposition and difference from which these films generate their dramatic energies' (1995: 2–10). Pfeil deliberately selects for examples popular and maximally accessible actioners (the 1987–1990 *Die Hard* and *Lethal Weapon* franchises) to argue that they operate on formal levels like 'certified Pomo art-films' disguised by 'straightforward plots' (*ibid*.).

Ernesto Acevedo-Muñoz keenly acknowledges 'selective patterning' in *Tu Mamá* akin to 'postmodern strategies' of a 'counterepic' but extrapolates these to gender and class politics more than acclimatizing the textual operations themselves (2004: 41). Comparably compelling readings recognize, for example, that *Tu Mamá*'s 'interstitial scenes' decenter the plot's attention to Mexican nationalism (Saldaña-Portillo 2005: 752), or its occasional 'cacophon[ies]' disrupt the narrative's 'smooth surface' to 'reveal historical sutures' (Lahr-Vivaz 2006: 80). Andrea Noble cautions viewers, particularly when confronted with contradictory moments, 'to take another look . . . at the whole question of looking' (2005: 141–6). Radical reflection prompted by *Tu Mamá*'s youthful address does precisely that.

Nuala Finnegan, examining global-local aspects of Mexican national identity, proves that *Tu Mamá* undermines its own oppositional constructs, resulting in 'a profound ambivalence evident at every level: character, camera work, plot, genre' (2007: 30–1). Julia Kroll distinctly recognizes a 'poststructuralist explosion of dialectic' akin to Adorno's negative dialectics as part of *Tu Mamá*'s '"experimental" narrative process and form' in direct refutation of Mexican national identity traditionally 'founded in oppositional binaries' (2007: 27–8). Notably, Kroll's reading does not limit itself to isolated themes but purposefully surveys them alongside 'time and spatial relations' (*ibid*.: 40).

*Tu Mamá* complicates post-classical frameworks through national and transnational gestures, which sometimes translate into themes inviting our interpretations. Frequently themes contest or outright contradict one another. And while these points remain valid if segregated from equally valid points in the film, I argue that the (post)structural network they form is more significant. Considering select influences helps explain how the film arrives at its intricately wrought stories (and ultimately lifts higher from them too) and will prove worth the journey.

Let us turn to the Godardian example. *Masculine Feminine* enacts a kind of tutor text for *Tu Mamá*. Its surface reveals a curious young-love story. Paul (Jean-Pierre Léaud) is both a want-to-be writer lost in archly delivered aphorisms and a want-to-be socialist revolutionary more committed to crude humor and immature angst. Madeleine (Chantal Goya) boasts an even shallower ignorance of public affairs and devotes herself to a rising career as a yé-yé singer. With three 20-something friends, they come to represent, famously, Godard's 'children of Marx and Coca-Cola,' a generation struggling with the transitions into early adulthood during an age caught amid political turmoil and global-corporate commercialism. Like in *Tu Mamá*, characters remain naïve, arrogant, and mostly unaware of their predicament. Pauline Kael celebrates *Masculine Feminine*'s young adults localized in mid-1960s Paris as 'this new breed in between teen-agers and people' with a 'beauty of youth that can endow Pop with poetry' (1966: 25–9), a critical line that easily foretells our *Charolastras*. Godard provides a cue toward something deep when he ruminates: *Masculine Feminine* is not 'about youth' as much as it is 'a philosophical idea . . . a way of reacting to things' (quoted in Daix 1966: 16–17).

The comparisons to *Tu Mamá* continue. *Masculine Feminine* announces its structure as '15 *faits précis*,' '15 specific events.' Its opening title card references the 'Manifesto of 121,' an anti-war proclamation, but the political point deflates as characters then model 'Pepsi Generation' *du jour* (Brody 2008: 263). Both films relate institutional-political transitions, Godard's occurring amidst the 1965 French presidential election, the nation's first direct vote for that office since the Second Republic in 1848 and a promise of democratic values through constitutional reform.

Shifting tones and highly stylized narration provide the most useful points of comparison. Both films differentiate character-subjective, diegetic-objective, synchronous-asynchronous, and heterodiegetic-authorial layers of information around the storytelling. One of Godard's methods operates largely through abstractions drawn out by title cards, typically silent but at least once spoken by a contrasting extradiegetic voice-over. Godard's voice-over technique invites greater ambiguity than clarity. Crucially unlike *Tu Mamá*, regular close-ups on characters frame them like portraits of ennui or confusion saturated with subjective quality. For example, sitting in a laundromat, Paul confesses, 'I don't know why I'm joking; actually I feel miserable.' Here and in a handful of significant moments, a character looks to the viewer in a direct-address acknowledgement that punctuates the narrative's shifting tones with the close-up one shot. The second-person address happens only once in *Tu Mamá*, at a crucial moment before the first of several reiterative 'climaxes' as Luisa in medium-full dances into the camera in the longest long take of the film.

*Masculine Feminine* also makes frequent use of long-take shots in accompaniment to its continuity-based editing and to follow its characters through extended action. The alternating stylistic pattern is not as rhythmically convoluted or systematically consistent as in *Tu Mamá*, I argue. What is up for question is not the quality of the film but the expectations brought to the viewing experience—and carried back out. That Bordwell, with immense expertise, fairly troubles over situating Godard's oeuvre across two classical-alternative modes—parametric cinema (the mode 'most controversial,' most problematic, and least understood) and a fourth ad hoc category (expressly for Godard's 'indeterminacy,' 'transtextuality,' and palimpsestic applications themselves)—speaks to the difficulty in analyzing narration that systematically redresses its own stylish aesthetics (1985: 274, 310–12). If parametric modality organizes films where stylistic patterns systematically exceed the efficiency of the storytelling, then it only partly explains the plot-style relationship in this montage as structuralism is dismantled, realigned, and usually revalorized to varying degrees (*ibid.:* 275). Godard describes his 'mélange' as 'a whole through fragments': 'each shot is not organized with respect to the dramatic function. A film is not a series of shots but an ensemble of shots' (quoted in Maillat 1965: 23). Elsewhere Godard explained the logic where 'two shots which follow each other do not necessarily follow each other' (1972: 215).

However enigmatic the explanations may seem, Alfonso Cuarón echoes Godard's parametric-informed logic when he articulates the general idea of, for instance, *Tu Mamá*'s characters meeting the military-style road blocks:

> part of the reason we see those *campesinos* [farmers] being stopped by the police is that Tenoch's father is politically corrupt, and because he is a corrupt politician, Tenoch is the way that he is. In a way, they are all products of that society.
>
> (quoted in Basoli 2002: 28)

If dismantling a corrupt, hypocritical, and paradoxical dominant structure requires a strange logic, then a strange logic may benefit from strange forms of expression and heuristics. Entertainment helps (even as it distracts), but the stranger the form of expression-perception, the more viewers must attune to the text for its full benefits. Loose associations may outperform deductive reasoning and lucidity between ideas. Ahead in 1999 Mexico City, we have Godard's generational counterparts in *Tu Mamá*—Cuarón's children of Zappa and Zapatistas.

'In the beginning, there was Zappa,' proclaims Alfonso Cuarón, the Biblical phrasing fairly tongue-in-cheek but also not to be overlooked (Anhelo

2002). The filmmakers recall sitting in their garden and exchanging ideas on *Tu Mamá*'s story with 'Watermelon in Easter Hay' playing:

> in an endless loop while we bounced ideas back and forth. And the loop kept on running until we finished the script, and later until we had the final cut of the film. . . . We owe so much to Zappa.
>
> (*ibid.*)

This song plays reverentially over the closing credits too, perhaps a subtle nod to artistic collaboration and inspiration. The title of the song invokes an absurd image, as Zappa muses, the 'miracle' of a 'musical event' blooming something 'unnatural or unknown or alien or beyond or scientific or whatever' (quoted in Swenson 2011). Art absurdly and divinely reinvents itself like fruit born inexplicably, its own mundane immaculate conception.

Redressing avant-garde symphonic music's total serialism into his rock, Zappa reconceives chord structures into what he calls a scale-permutated 'stack of sounds,' not infrequently mixing in disquieting found-art noises (quoted in Menn et al. 1992). Further, and not unlike Godard's parametric narration, Zappa's music strategically deconstructs the rhythm-pitch duality of traditional song forms (*ibid.*). These (post)structurally experimental qualities compare with *Tu Mamá*'s exceptionally convoluted soundtrack, intermingling subtle but distinct volumetric and contrapuntal qualities and visuals, yielding a specially sequenced stack of images.

Frequently Zappa's rock music utilizes a recitative *sprechstimme*, which surely informs *Tu Mamá*'s voice-over technique and heterodiegetic identifications. *Tu Mamá* and 'Watermelon in Easter Hay' brandish curious, raucous, even scatological themes, but these cannot be individuated as they coalesce around inspiring and transcendent messages in their reformative aesthetics. At least one Zappa scholar likens this to Adorno's negative dialectics, whereby negative values, not synthesis, result from an alternative-dialectical paradigm (Watson 1995). Zappa names the effect 'xenochrony,' 'strange synchronizations' (1987; Marshall 1988).

Unlike 'normal' musical composition and engineering that, like cinema's classicism, strive for smoothly 'invisible' style, equating to 'normative' production value and presumed mainstream tastes, xenochrony assembles and systematically fuses varying parts precisely to emphasize their disunified, multi-textured whole. For Zappa, the assemblage resituates innovative contiguity or slight or temporary juxtaposition for a song's foundation; on top of that, another 'part' (sometimes explicitly musical, sometimes expressionistically associational) operates atonally and/or quasi-rhythmically or counter-rhythmically.

Narratologically, these strange combinations result in a 'conceptual continuity' replete with its own strange logic (Carr 2013a: 12–15; Menn et al. 1992). As Paul Carr notes, the conceptual continuity paradigms enable Zappa 'to manipulate time, space, and place in an unusually consistent manner' (2013b: 142). Zappa's music celebrates dissonance. Rather than resolving it, he vaunts, 'most of the time I just leave it squatting there' (quoted in Menn et al. 1992). Zappa proclaims 'conceptual continuity' achieves phenomenal 'rhythmic relationships unachievable by other means'—something like *experiencing* 'Monday and Tuesday crammed into the space of Wednesday' (1987).

'Watermelon in Easter Hay' epitomizes xenochrony as both complex song and sequenced *denouement* for the three-act youth-story *Joe's Garage* (1979). The rock opera features a trance-like voice as mock-bureaucratic 'Central Scrutinizer,' a hypodiegetic narrator who discerns that the main character Joe, stuck amid teenage frenzy, depression, and sexual frustration, has 'realized' that 'imaginary guitar notes and imaginary vocals exist only in the imagination of the imaginer.' With 'imaginer' dissipating in volume, a rhythm-bass sequence alternates between four and five beats, like marching left-right-left-right but stumbling on the last step. This loops; pacing hampers momentum; the song advances steadily unsteadily. Voice-over narration murmurs against multiply textured whispers, heavy breathing, and laughs to introduce our 'imaginary solo.' (And this is where things get 'stranger.')

Curiously mixing technical precision, creative fluidity, and mysticism, Zappa's virtuosic electric guitar soars above the already multi-textured layers of this song. The astounding seven-minute solo likely distracts listeners from the systematically consistent sequencing and its disarming effects. Zappa's multi-textured aesthetics counteract artistic and social structures for processual listening experiences. Informed by *Masculine Feminine* and 'Watermelon in Easter Hay,' *Tu Mamá* manipulates the structural experiments into maximally accessible mythologies of youth.

Transitions between Acts One and Two in *Tu Mamá* demonstrate parametric style and conceptual continuity. After our trio has met at Tenoch's sister's wedding and Julio and Tenoch have made their sophomoric attempt at romancing Luisa, the offer to go on the beach trip remains both unanswered and answered. That is, Luisa answers that she and her husband '*va a encantar*,' 'will love' to go, but she probably also means that, at the same time, as a sarcastic refusal. Her contradictory answer is dismissive because it mocks polite conversation and manners of cordiality. And yet the issue—going to the beach—remains unresolved. Will they go to Boca del Cielo? A series of consecutive scenes reflect at first glance a set of actions that seem, if viewers ignore the contested values around the first invitation, relatively reasonable to follow:

1. Luisa calls Tenoch to ask if the 'invitation is still open' for the beach trip;
2. Tenoch makes the arrangement with Luisa;
3. Tenoch calls Julio;
4. Tenoch and Julio visit with Julio's sister to negotiate use of Betsabé;
5. they shop for beer, snacks, and condoms;
6. they consult Saba on travel directions;
7. Julio and Tenoch pick up Luisa;
8. our group embarks on the trip together.

Never mind that this grouping appears most incredible from the start, even based directly on the characters' own invitation and response. The suggestion of a clear-cut linear causality—one phone call to the next, one arrangement with the next—as well as the idiotic playfulness of Julio and Tenoch together probably disarm viewers. Unreflective readings likely default to classical paradigm rules—but lose out in the translations. More, each character has personal investments but only partly betrays them across the arrangements. Thematic cues and linear-forward action mask the sequence's complexity. Julio and Tenoch likely hope for rambunctious adventure and a purpose for the condoms. Luisa acknowledges later that she knows this is what the 'two wanted from the start' but comes to seek grander aspirations of self-actualization balanced with care for them. Viewers wonder, too, how much, for example, the excursion to the Zapatista-inspired demonstration and the stakes Manuela, Julio's sister as 'minor' character, might supply the advancing storyline. Worse, some viewers find disappointment in not directly learning *enough* about Manuela and her causes, expecting or wanting more. Loose connections and tactful threading are typical for feature films, and yet *Tu Mamá* advantages 'looseness' more than films accommodating classical paradigm regulation. The form deserves scrutiny.

This sequence actually intermingles a relatively wide range of tones from adolescent playfulness and drug-induced laxity to adult reserved, even prim, demeanor. More crucially, the sequence aligns for comparison six settings of relevance to our story introduction but also ranging across public-private realms, political values, and economic class bases—from upper-class affluence to middle-class and academic to thoroughly working-class. The characters' more-or-less private lives collide with the larger world and variegated social conditions they all live in. And most crucial of all, a sequential chain presents this storyline and situates these ideas through stylistically alternating patterns that partly serve but also exceed viewers' accessibility to the text.

Consider the first phone call. Five shots depict Leo, Tenoch's nanny, walking from the kitchen and through the expansive family home on her way to deliver him his favorite snack. With durations of 5, 7, 12, and 12 seconds, the action incrementally builds to the anchor of a 35-second long take on Tenoch lounging on an upstairs couch in a family media room [see Figure 3.1]. The soundtrack is texturally complex, as diegetic sounds of workers in the kitchen, an indoor courtyard fountain, and Leo's footsteps play against an already heavily layered but rhythmically unified hip-hop song by Titán featuring Mala Rodríguez, all while the phones ring in tandem throughout the house.

The rhythms of the soundtrack abrade the pace of the editing and perforate the continuity of the visuals across the scene. A transparent classical style would depict this story more singularly, and the representations would tend to resolve things like affluent *or* nurturing home, Leo as loving nanny *or* domestic helper, Tenoch as pampered teen *or* politically active young adult, etc., to hold respective values more securely. Instead, the issues are confused by an art form that exposes itself, the social structures it conveys, and their values. One result is that viewers must choose along a spectrum of access points to align with *and* resist the text. We never anchor fully into Leo's or Tenoch's perspective, for example, and yet the cinema language and alternative-dialectics help viewers to assess *and* empathize across their different positions across contingent circumstances.

*Figure 3.1* Privilege and Devotion Quietly Tested

Redressing our sense of continuity formally rather than strictly diegetically and thematically, this scene's ubiquitous phone ringing reverts palimpsestically to the dial tone-turned-sobbing wails from the previous moment as Luisa hung up on Jano's drunken confession. Visuals collide from Luisa alone in darkened bedroom to the palatial family home. Now the phone, within arm's reach of Tenoch, rings at least eight times before Leo answers, which might be as clear of a sign of his privilege in this environment as the surrounding material objects and size of the home. Unaware, Tenoch sports a Subcomandante Marcos shirt ironically against cuffed lounging pants and cushiony slippers. The socialist-revolutionary icon, for example, appears here and can be read as such fairly directly, but its relationship to the complex of visual and aural images likely leaves larger questions blatantly unanswered. And the film performs these types of stylistic maneuvers consistently and systematically.

Though affectionate with one another, Leo wipes the phone clean before deferentially handing it to Tenoch. Background-center, a framed image of Our Lady suggests a reflection of Leo. Maternal and devotional care battles with class-, race-, and economy-based values in the action. Simplified continuity glosses these for narrative development, but conceptual continuity exposes the implied structures to question the net of implicated values. Nonetheless, viewers move *forward* because the narrative advances. The conceptual continuity of this first scene contrasts sharply with a 35-second long take at Luisa's more brightly lit and lightly colored apartment, a 66-second long take at Julio's very utilitarian and working-class family apartment, and a 24-second long take as Julio and Tenoch weave through CGH protestors to locate his sister. Noticeably shifting the pace, the sequence continues with the supermarket scene consisting of five much quicker shots with durations of 3.5 to 6 seconds each. The sequence continues with two shots of Saba's apartment, where two of his girlfriends braid hair and share a bong in the background while the guys discuss travel directions in mid and foreground. The sequence concludes with Luisa packed and joining Tenoch and Julio (and Betsabé) to begin their journey (and Act Two) together.

Viewers adhering to classical paradigm readings likely at this point want to 'make sense' of the story elements, probably strive to and can make some sense of much of individual parts, but still these add up to partial truths that leave the rest in question. What is the sum? Why are there remainders? Why so many partial truths and remainders? It would be a mistake to write this off simply as a poorly crafted story. Equations exceed the dramaturgy. The alternating sequencing of long takes and subtly unconventional continuity editing combine with sounds for a complicated montage that seems to riddle the presumed linear-causality of many actions (e.g., one phone call to the next, arrangements for the trip).

Over the last 15 seconds of the shot in Julio's family apartment, the camera turns away from him urinating and saunters past family photographs and down a wall to an open window. Our tenth voice-over entry narrates Julio's family background. His father's long absence and abandoning the family dialectically matches with his single mother's absence due to long work hours. According to the narrator, she has 'worked all her life as a secretary in a multi-national corporation.' A sewing machine stays ready for mending family wares after 'work,' and our view lands on neighboring project housing.

After a brief pause, the visuals cut to the CGH march while the voice-over explains that Betsabé served as collateral for Julio's and his sister's 'tense negotiations.' Julio and Tenoch make the trip with Luisa, and Manuela later will deliver 'food, clothing, and medicine' to activists in Chiapas. This roughly 39-second voice entry figures collaterally with the long-take cinematography and subtly revised continuity cut between the two shots to exceed the logical connections of phone calls and trip arrangements. Rather than focusing on any one issue directly (e.g., corporate consumerism, socio-economic class, family values, political protest, social activism, etc.), the stylized narration recognizes the structures maintaining the issues and invites our processual-experiential questioning across them.

*Tu Mamá* erodes the distinctions between 'major' and 'minor' characters, main story and 'digressions,' and the full array of competing realities and values that inform this millennial condition. Chronotopic and other story elements help formulate realities that cannot accommodate one another but nonetheless must coexist. The alternating and utterly systematic stylistic patterns across this and every sequence in *Tu Mamá* subtly evinces the structures—first artistic-representational structures and as a result comparably conventional social structures—and the values they maintain. Strategically images *follow* one another in multiple ways, and remainders *squat there* for viewers to consider. Viewing *Tu Mamá* affords a range of experiences that open up to processes of change.

Let us add in Žižek. By 2007 in *Possibility of Hope*, Žižek begins making actual screen appearances, but his philosophical influence is assuredly present before that. Describing *Children of Men* as a 'remake' 'in a strange way' of *Tu Mamá*, Žižek points to what he calls a 'paradox of anamorphosis' (2006a). Literally a form or structure turning back onto itself, anamorphosis occurs when a part of a picture, viewed in one direct stance, first appears distorted and less meaningful than the straightforward parts; then, through another less direct stance, the distorted part clarifies itself and, thus, redresses meanings from the initial viewing experience. For Cuarón's films, Žižek explains that 'if you look at the Thing too directly . . . you don't see it,' but 'you can see it in an oblique way only if it remains in the background' (*ibid.*). A 'wonderful tension between foreground and background' para-doxically conceals, reveals, and reseats the significant differences among these layers of the film (plot and story, theme and form) (2006a, 2014). Focusing solely on the foreground, looking at *Tu Mamá* 'superficially,' Žižek cautions, a viewer will see the film as merely an adolescent 'sexual adventure' with selective themes (class, gender, nationalism, etc.) tied to the main characters and their stark differences; however, 'looking awry,' comparable to radically reflecting through cinematic address, and recognizing the complex relationships around treatment of our major and minor characters and their surroundings, viewers will find a 'prism' refracting the parts into a sharper image (2006a, 1991, 2014). This more holistic reading regularly supersedes *Tu Mamá*'s allegorical frameworks without invalidating them.

Equally important, and also paradoxical, anamorphic viewing positions hybridize objective and subjective conceptions of perspective and agency. If reality initially appears as a construction of 'actual' arrangements, the anamorphic 'stain' problematizes it, destabilizes what seemed stable (and pleasing in its conformity), and moves the viewers to look again and reposition the situation at hand (Žižek 2006a). Repositioning applies to questions of social values held in check by the constructions.

Žižek illustrates experiential-processual aspects of the repositioning by describing denizens on different edges of a community who draw maps of their shared space differently (2006b: 25–6). The differences, he elucidates, point to not merely location nor cultural relativism, but more crucially 'social antagonism' that aims (and fails in large measure) to impose a 'balanced symbolic structure' (*ibid.*). The shared 'vision of reality' contradicts itself by showing 'simultaneously the Thing to which direct access is not possible and the obstacle which prevents the direct access,' but it also may disclose a hidden reference point or implied constant (2006b: 25–6, 1991: 11–12). The 'split' 'seems irreducible,' 'cannot be resolved via a higher "dialectical synthesis,"' and elevates society into an inaccessible Thing-in-itself' (2006b: 26). The Real 'is ultimately the very shift of perspectives from the first standpoint to the second,' a perspectival process that is necessarily intersubjective (*ibid.*). Fantasy stages these transidentifying desires.

Recall the opening sequence of the film. The initial image emphasizes a hallway passage with a darkened wall in foreground. Sexual action appears abstractly around a corner and in the background, which viewers discern according to the walking hand-held camera repositioning the view on the engaged teens. Cinematography enacts the anamorphic phenomenon. Interpretations anticipating classical style focus so intently on deciphering sexual actions they may neglect the condition surrounding these characters-in-environment in favor of the insinuated sensationalism of the scene. Upon repositioned reflection, the film's style draws new attention not solely to foregrounded information nor backgrounds but to both and integrally to the very structures holding issues and their values in place. Following chapters continue to apply these frameworks.

Anamorphosis, ascribed abstractly more than applied graphically, may also help explain (or alleviate the need to discern definitively) the naming throughout this film.[1] Nicknames and slurs create their own referential category, but many of our characters, major and minor, have highly evocative names. Julio's surname Zapata references Emiliano Zapata and the succeeding generations of revolutionary movements, Mexican Revolution 1910–1920 and EZLN (Zapatista Army) since 1994, but Julio hardly fits such a militant-socialist model neatly. Tenoch's surname Iturbide references Augustín I, criollo-royalist general in Mexico's War of Independence 1810–1821 and the nation's First Regency President and Constitutional Emperor in 1821–1822. Tenoch references the founder of the Aztec-Mexica city-state Tenochtitlán in 1325, and our character was named in a conspicuous (if antistrophic) gesture by his politician father, as our fourth voice-over narrator entry discloses, 'infected (*contagiado*) by a sudden urge of nationalism.' The son was originally to be named Hernán, an easy reference to Cortés, the Spanish conquistador most associated with overthrowing the indigenous empire and destroying Tenochtitlán in 1521. Luisa's last name being Cortés references both conqueror and his relationship to *la Malinche*, legendary mother of Mexican mestizaje. The competing interpretations of *la Malinche* as seductress, traitor, and oppressed victim may overlap with the name given to the car the trio ride in, *Betsabé* or Bathsheba, and those Biblical overtones. Among four 'main' characters' names a bizarre chain forms.

Seemingly 'minor' characters carry equally evocative references through their naming. Chuy's full name, Jesús Carranza, for example, not only obviously offers an association with the Christian Messiah but combines this with Mexican political references to Venustiano Carranza, the Constitutionalist *primer jefe* 1913–1917 and Mexican President 1917–1920. Carranza's father, Jesús, also served in Mexico's army and allied Benito Juárez, who will make a later appearance. There are more examples. What can viewers make of these painstakingly referential names, especially as they do not make thoroughly clear connections with symbolic readings of the characters nor neat allegorical revelations? When Luisa asks if the 'beautiful names' of the beaches she hopes to visit mean anything, the film teases viewers with a slack answer: 'who knows.'

Anamorphosis suggests a hint. More important than names are 'backgrounds.' Viewers learn fairly late in Act Two from our narrator that all *four* of our travelers experienced profound moments of growth in their youth, distinguished expressedly by a 'pang' that combines physical pain with emotional agitation. After Julio sees Tenoch and Luisa having sex, and just before the second swimming race, hypodiegetic voice-over explains that 'Julio couldn't understand' his feelings and experiential knowledge: 'He knew it wasn't rage. The only other time he'd felt this pain in his gut was when he was eight' and discovered by accident 'his mother in his godfather's arms.' After swimming but with wins and losses not fully calculated, Julio then confesses/boasts his sexual infidelity with Tenoch's girlfriend Ana, and the narrator provides a matching explanation that Tenoch is overcome by a similar adolescent confusion and pang: 'Tenoch had only felt this pain in his gut when he was 11, when he saw his father's picture in an article linking him to a scandal involving the sale of contaminated corn to the poor.'

It is too simplistic and romantic to merely name these a 'loss of innocence'; and yet the film prompts us, initially, to decipher story events this way but then also re-examine them (Žižek 2014). These stories have in common family dynamics and betrayals but also engage larger social customs and values. Moreover, the film treats these profound moments of growth through intricately stylized aural-visual narration that affords viewers both diffused empathy with the characters as well as a critical stance against them and the conditions they 'couldn't understand' (yet). Backgrounds systemically refocus foregrounds.

Luisa's background reveals similar, reiteratively comparative experiential moments of profound growth. The Cuaróns' screenplay relates that as a very young girl Luisa saw her mother after a Sunday mass give alms to one poor man but then overlook a second poor man; her conscience was struck, and she felt '*una punzada aguda arriba del estómago*,' 'a sharp pang in her stomach' (*ibid.*: 37–8). She consciously sacrificed one principle of not stealing for the sake of what she believed to be the greater principle of charity. The following Sunday, she stole 100 pesetas and gave them to this man to restore 'balance' (*ibid.*).

Some may be surprised by the insistence of reading the station wagon as a fourth character, but not only does her naming-to-background ratio compare with our human trio, but she even experiences consciousness and, with several parallels to Luisa especially, demonstrates her own sense of conscience. Not just factory-produced but '*nació*,' 'born,' explained playfully in the Cuaróns' screenplay, in Hidalgo, Mexico, the 1983 Chrysler Le Baron's material form certainly embodies national/transnational values linked to class, political economy, family, luxury, privilege, and more (*ibid.*: 51). Parts of her background provide a prism by which immateriality refocuses the material items and their subscribed values.

Betsabé learns of sex—through rite of passage as much as for her human companions—when her drivers engage in indiscreet but liberating roadside 'quickies' (*ibid.*: 52, 57). The vibrancy of sexuality and young life travels with the harsh reality of death for our foursome. Betsabé experiences her own 'panged' moment of profound growth when she accidentally was driven over a small dog. The sight and sound details from her perspective are visceral as 'crushing ribs "cronch,"' the body rolls and drags underneath briefly, and Betsabé feels overcome by 'an irritating tickle in her crankcase and along her exhaust pipe' (*ibid.*: 52). Betsabé's conscience is struck by an awareness of mortality and suffering, which reemerges as a 'chilled shiver' every time something brushes against her chassis, recalling the 'sensation of death' (*ibid.*). When Julio first learns that Ceci is leaving for Italy, Betsabé seems to understand Julio's jealousy and abandonment better than he does himself; or perhaps the suggestion is that viewers might come to understand characters' feelings precisely through unconventional perspectives and unorthodox means (*ibid.*: 57).

Incomplete associations around naming and backstories may demonstrate the distance between our histories and the historiography behind them. And yet the histories transport values across the times they treat. Another related possibility considers how individuals entering ritualized transformation are both denied their names and renamed for their liminal personae undergoing processes of growth—'at once no longer classified and not yet classified' (Turner 1967: 96). Ceremonies structure the events in exquisitely social terms. Consolidating the first two possibilities is that these references and associations act like appositives, literally a grammatical renaming of a person or thing that points to merely facets and not the whole.

Like the 'grammatical example' Barthes discusses for mythology, characteristics might be appropriative and distortive in die-casting an image; the overall effect of naming, character description, even chronotope draws viewers into complicity, an 'alibi' for correlative values (2012: 233–5). Like synecdoche, the facet stands associatively for the whole and symbolically accentuates (even overdetermines) that facet's contingent function for the whole (which both seems rational and admits its own artificiality or arbitrariness). And as is always the case, remaining facets go unnoticed. In anamorphic terms, not only should viewers pay fuller attention to the parts normally gone less noticed but perhaps reimagine those prismatically for clearer understandings of the complex situation.

A less obvious, equally puzzling, but all the more rewarding example of *Tu Mamá*'s anamorphic riddle lies in diegetic space.[2] One would need a magical cartography to map the entire trip that this film suggests. At start, there are clear, sometimes excruciatingly clear, geographic and temporal references to events in Mexico City—the airport; the CGH protest near the Angel of Independence monument; the Lienzo Charro del Pedregal; even the *supermercado* opposite Saba's neo-hippy apartment. These match loosely with ritual-ceremonial or at least highly symbolic events like trust in friendship, long goodbyes to loved ones, respect for the departed, public demonstrations of political activism, modern consumerism, weddings, first meetings and greetings, and parties. Following the *desviación* (both diversion and deviation) from the '*directo*' highway and to the Oaxaca '*libre*' (both toll-free and unbridled) road, the journey meets (literally and figuratively) a *peregrinación*/pilgrimage, and the route begins encumbering some of the confusion but mind-bending liberty of Saba's directions. Adding to the confusion, maps appear in the screenplay that seem to document toponymy, topography, even highway markers for *Tu Mamá*'s trip, but projection-representation is askew, and they include incongruities against conventional Mexican road maps (Cuarón and Cuarón 2001: 60–1, 118–19, 202–3, 236–7).

The trio's first meal together and night's stay occurs in a location identified as Xochiapa. This name most directly references a small, historical town in Veracruz that, combining history and mythic identification, was founded in the 17th century by Zapotec Indians in exile and over the centuries remains heavily contextualized in protectionist-isolationist indigenous cultural values. And yet, Veracruz lies far east of a reasonably expected 'México-Puebla-Oaxaca' route (Cuarón and Cuarón 2001: 118–19). Moreover, because this sequence is filmed in Oaxaca City, around Guelaguetza's restaurant and lodge, the story depicts an urban and diverse community north of Tepelmeme, which appears somewhat strangely out the passenger side of Betsabé, westward of their southern movement. Travelling south on Mexico's highway system the next morning, one reasonably expects Tepelmeme Villa de Morales toward the east, visible out their driver's side of the car. If the route is not enchanted, then at least it leads in multiply indirect and often confusing or confused but promising pathways.

Further down the road too, visiting Teposcolula, where Luisa meets Doña Martiña and Betsabé gets repaired, requires a double-back north and certainly is not a 'direct' route toward the beach. Again, screenplay notes situate this in linear travel *forward* (*ibid.*). Is this story steering in circles? Even if so, this visit delivers our characters opportunities for testing their maturity and proving (or disproving) their growth. Youthful sexuality serves keenly here for some explanation.

Julio and Tenoch initially invent Boca del Cielo; they know (or believe) at the start of their trip that it does not actually exist ('*no existe*'); they nonetheless follow directions from Saba; with Luisa, they arrive; ultimately all discover a place fully recognized as such. Fairly no conventional logic can consolidate those five facts of the story, yet the narrative strings them together. Playful tones and presumed 'sexiness' likely distract viewers further over the story's arc. Upon retrospection, the significance of travel throughout this film's spatio-temporal reality derives less from object-level truths and more from intuitive transformational possibilities. Associational 'backgrounds' redress explicit foregrounds. Less than actual, manifest, places and senses of being, the travel mobilizes experiences for becoming.

The combinations of 'facts' do not entirely refute the film's ostensible 'realism' nor ontological bases; to the contrary, the realistic-material aspects of this storyworld, which often secure classical paradigm-based interpretations, here invite useful confusion and radical retrospection. Viewers may surrender (as Tenoch and Julio do by return to Mexico City) or begin to imagine anew (as Luisa claims in her after-life). Manifestations of being and processes of becoming reside in between the options.

## Notes

1. A range of readings on character naming includes Acevedo-Muñoz (2004), Lahr-Vivaz (2006: 80), Saldaña-Portillo (2005: 762, 776 n28), and Benson-Allott (2009).
2. Wide disparities exist on understanding story space and place; see, for example, Lie (2017: 69–73), Díaz (2005), Serna (2004), Menne (2007: 80), Worrell (2011: 162, 158), and Oropesa (2008: 97–100).

# 4 'The *Charolastra* Manifesto'

| | | |
|---|---|---|
| 1. | *No hay honor más grande que ser un Charolastra.* | There's no greater honor than being a *Charolastra*. |
| 2. | *Cada quien hace de su culo un papalote.* | Do whatever the fuck you feel like. |
| 3. | *Pop mata poesía.* | Pop beats poetry. |
| 4. | *Un toque al día, la llave de la alegría.* | Getting high once a day keeps the doctor away. |
| 5. | *No te tirarás a la vieja de otro Charolastra.* | Thou shalt not screw another *Charolastra's* girl. |
| 6. | *Puto el que le vaya al América.* | Team América is for fags. |
| 7. | *¡Que muera la moral! ¡Que viva la chaqueta!* | Whacking off rules. |
| 8. | *Prohibido casarse con una virgen.* | Never marry a virgin. |
| 9. | *Puto el que le vaya al América (se repite porque es reputo el que le vaya al América).* | Team América is for fags. (It bears repeating.) |
| 10. | *La neta es chida pero inalcanzable.* | Truth is cool, but unattainable. |
| 11. | *Pierde la calidad de Charolastra el culero que rompa cualquiera de los puntos anteriores.* | The asshole who breaks any of the above rules forfeits the title of '*Charolastra*.' |

Julio and Tenoch with three friends formulate this manifesto statement and the appellation *Charolastra*. Naming throughout this film, in the adolescent self-identifying case of the *Charolastras* here and as mentioned earlier for so many names, accumulates in multivalence and eventually collapses under its own referential weight. *Charolastra* is a neologism combining Spanish words for 'space cowboy.' Keener than in previous conversations, Julio explains to Luisa the transferential quality of the puns on '*astral*' and '*lastre*,' ethereal and cosmic but equally a ballast or burden (which subtitles simplify to the point of erasing the xenochronic-dialectical point). In the wedding scene, the *charros* carry Eurocentric connotations of a horseman serving nobility, and the Cuarón brothers' glossary notes that '*charolas*' also alludes to Mexican identity cards (2001: 244). Pointedly, the glossary refrains from simply defining 'Charolastra' itself, leaving that open for conjecture.

Before Julio and Tenoch deliver the manifesto line-by-line to Luisa early in their road trip, they explain that the term derived from their friend Daniel's misunderstanding of the English-language lyrics to a popular rock song, 'All Star' by Smash Mouth (*ibid*.: 197 n28).

The derivation and naming of our group and its manifesto are based on misunderstood facts and partial truths; they revolve around the tensions over inclusivity-exclusivity, advocacy-judgment, and intimacy-distance the film has offered from the start with little resolution or synthesis.

Word choice in the manifestos presents many problems even for Spanish-speaking audiences, and subtitling ensiles competing interpretations. 'Whacking off rules' misses the declamatory colloquialism of '¡*que viva!*' and its traditional festive and memorializing qualities but with pun on 'long-living' admiration. 'Thou shalt' may overdress the *Chilango* slang but not the irony of exalted 'honor' and accompanying principles built into the manifesto genre. Like so many parts of this film where tones mix, the manifesto proclamations draw out xenochronic-strange combinations precisely to disclose larger hypocrisies and contradictions. Among other things, a reiterative dialogue between the two manifestos in this film debates *pronouncements of being* compared to *processes of becoming*.

That '*puto*' translates in subtitles as 'fags' unquestionably calls out homophobic machismo in Julio and Tenoch, and yet they express support and advocacy for their coming-out gay friend Daniel. They 'hardly ever see' Daniel since he is 'into other scenes,' but according to the subtitles 'he's still in the club.' The subtitling translation dreadfully oversimplifies the competition among nationalist-heteronormative values and also misses the pluralistic identification and inclusivity that the dialogue suggests: '*seguimos siendo carnalitos*,' literally 'we continue *being* brothers' (cf. *ibid*.: 128). (And rather than the stricter '*hermanos*' for 'brothers,' '*carnalitos*' connotes an endearing 'of the same flesh' in its long-standing slang usage.) One girl, Pecas, is only an 'honorary' *Charolastra* because, according to Tenoch, she dates 'sucky boyfriends' and (or?) because, according to Julio, she refused to sign their manifesto. Who refused whom and in what degrees of honor and friendship? It is frequently unclear the extent to which these points are collateral truths or competing claims, all shaped by unacknowledged biases. Mock seriousness disguises intelligibility around these messages, yet the narration invites radical reflection.

Even as they define '*Charolastra*' in turns and in unison, Tenoch and Julio contradict themselves and hint at deeper incompatibility. Subtitling offers that 'it was really Saba who came up with' the term while tripping on mushrooms. The script clarifies that Julio, speaking quietly from the back seat, interjects that Saba's pun on 'charola' refers (also? more directly?) to the identity card of Tenoch's father, a high-level official in the national current-ruling party, PRI. Family privilege trickles down to Tenoch and sometimes his friends but coincides with abuses of power and corruption. Luisa doesn't pursue the point. Tenoch dodges this glancing blow and emphasizes instead the equally true points that Saba increasingly experiments with drug-induced altered states, so his ideas are sometimes unclear. Yet it is Saba, the post-punk supertramp, whom they turn to and trust for directions and trip planning.

The *Charolastras* form an adolescent group already heading different directions into adulthood; Julio and Tenoch just do not realize it (yet). Luisa, more aware, asks if they will share their manifesto with her. Playfully they refuse—and then do it anyway. Like make-believe spies revealing a 'top secret,' according to the subtitles, the pact is even more symbolically described by Tenoch's line '*firmado con sangre*,' 'signed in blood.' And Julio mimics *Top Gun* (Scott 1986): we could tell you, but then 'we'd have to kill you.' Whimsical jokes, by film's end, these lines will prove haunting, given Luisa's death and the gravity of her lessons for them.

Over the 145-second long take, Julio and Tenoch deliver—nay, performatively proclaim in carnivalesque fashion—the manifesto line by line. Captured by camera-eye levitating alongside their moving car, the view remains slightly higher than eye-level and large enough both to see all three human reactions and to remain outside of singular perspectives [see Figure 4.1]. Viewers cannot focalize clearly with Tenoch and Julio as

*Figure 4.1* Delivery and Reception of 'The *Charolastra* Manifesto' Conflate Perspectives . . .

authors and chanters of the arguments, nor with Luisa's reception of them. At times the shot emphasizes Betsabé carrying them down the road, but the stageline shifts (smoothly and enough to 're-establish' the action). The shot's size, angle, and movement do not emphasize clear objectivity either. Agency and counter-agency both marry and compete throughout this long take as an address that unveils signifying operations for de-structured considerations of in-formation identities. Launching into the recitation of the manifesto, the group passes a '*peregrinación*,' a small caravan in pilgrimage [see Figure 4.2], and one significant associational quality of our trio's journey seems assured. If they are on pilgrimage, Boca del Cielo enacts a sacred destination. Proving their identities along the way requires votive purposes and sacrifices of the highest orders.

Per-item this manifesto reveals its own ironic dispositions. 'Do whatever you feel like' cancels out the entire notion of a pact or set of rules. Several manifesto arguments cast the kinds of in-formation opinions exemplary of teenage years, but a thread of trust and loyalty runs through them. That our *Charolastras* have already broken these rules—sexual infidelity topmost—proves the manifesto's ineffectiveness and falseness. An inherently corrupt document, the manifesto aligns with other instances of social corruption and hypocrisy throughout the story. Julio and Tenoch disqualify for the 'honor' built into it and lose entitlements manifestly ensured by it. According to Alfonso Cuarón, the manifesto represents a false stability, 'an absolute truth that does not exist,' and figuring this out is 'a painful process' for our characters (quoted in Fernández 2001).

*Figure 4.2* ... The Long Take's Stageline Re-establishes, and the Group Encounters Pilgrimages

Of greatest relevance to our interpretations is the resounding philosophical point, about which Luisa inquires: 'truth is cool, but unattainable.' This will reverberate with the narrator's disclosure to conclude this sequence. Our 12th voice-over entry cuts in for the last 16 seconds of the long take and bridges the continuity of our trio traveling in their first day and then arriving in Xochiapa for their first meal together and first night's rest. Like several narrator entries—at Luisa's doctor's office, the CGH demonstration, the cow pasture during a roadside break, and the country club pool with sprinklers— the hypodiegetic voice-over is lightly textured by hushed diegetic sounds. Here, synchronous low-volume sounds of Betsabé in motion, town ambience, and their braking stop at the restaurant/lodge texture the soundtrack against the long take resequenced into conceptual continuity. Upon radical reflection, the style displaces conventional expectations and, as a result, raises up for question the 'normative' values being represented. These permutations are subtle but significantly perturbatious.

In between storyworld and absolute objectivity, the narrator delivers unquestionably the most important set of ideas for viewers to consider; these are crucial for understanding not just the characters, especially Julio and Tenoch, but also the relationships they all share with their environments. The relationships are defined by the social conditions, modes of existence, and even ever-after existential concerns. More a codex for the *Charolastras'* *modus operandi* than the manifesto itself is, this set of ideas equally operates as *modus operandi* for interpreting *Tu Mamá*'s youthful address.

The narrator explains that the manifesto items derive from a larger universe with 'lots of other stories,' many of which they will share with Luisa over their shared journey:

> Each one reaffirmed the strong ties uniting them, the bond that created a solid indivisible entity. Their stories, though adorned by personal mythologies, were the truth. But as always happens, it was a partial truth. Much was omitted.

The examples offered for this principle might seem gratuitous and somewhat vulgar but are thoroughly mundane. Moreover, their determining structures, which are easily taken for granted, conflate social convention, economic class, political identity, and ethics. *Tu Mamá*'s address exposes these and calls them into question. Julio at Tenoch's house lights a match after using the bathroom to hide personal smells; Tenoch at Julio's house lifts the toilet seat with a foot to avoid the grossness; similar 'details they didn't need to know about each other' or choose to share all fill in gaps around the partial truths and competing realities that envelop them.

In spite of their friendship and youthful similarities—and manifesto co-authorship and duo performance—Julio occasionally exhibits less in common with Tenoch through classed distinctions than he does with Leo. Yet Julio gladly skims off of Tenoch's family's corrupt privilege whenever possible. Sometimes they use their differences as weapons against one another. Significantly, at other times Tenoch and Julio remain ignorant of or choose to ignore their differences—or further differences with, for example, Marcelino Escutia dead in the roadway, Doña Martina and residents of Teposcolula during Betsabé's breakdown, and the many lives that surround theirs that make up the many realities of Mexico. *Tu Mamá* encompasses them in mythologies of youth.

Through Luisa and her altruistic but gravely in-crisis identity, the journey inspires the adolescents to share more honesty and greater empathy around these details than they likely would have without the experiences together. Intimacies and sexual matters decode much of this. There are possibilities to learn from one another, to grow from their richer relationships, and there are new conflicts that arise in the disclosures. That 12th voice-over disclosure hinges with the 18th voice-over entry after Julio and Tenoch each recognizes his own very personal 'pang' of betrayal. From their universe of stories, they 'twist those details to create a less painful truth,' and then they seek out 'every possible detail' and try 'to put together a puzzle from pieces that didn't always fit.' And so do viewers recognizing this film's riddles.

As the first proclamation states explicitly, the objective of this manifesto is to pronounce 'being a *Charolastra*.' Put bluntly, manifestos as a genre articulate the existence of its arguments and frequently its authors, making them 'manifest.' The mere appearance invokes long-standing cinema traditions, which Chapter 7 explores materially. Initially, the 'being' of the *Charolastras* reflects this particular group of adolescents determining their adult identities with an arrogant presumption of knowledge. Little in its articles allows for disagreements with its competitive, say militant, stances or compromise with unified conceptions of 'being.'

There are ample gestures toward extrapolating the immaturity Tenoch and Julio exhibit with the Mexican nation-state or global regionalism at cruxes of development up to the turn to the 21st century, but these appear incomplete. Perhaps the most fruitful interpretive gestures, first, recognize the confusion and contradictions around the film's presentation of the manifesto and align those with similar aspects of the larger environments that characters inhabit. Second, because the film depicts these in subtly but deliberately unconventional ways, viewers can interrogate the social mechanisms being represented and the values they maintain. Finally, viewers may imagine themselves in a shifting landscape: by the time Luisa delivers her manifesto, which is more negotiably transactional than *Charolastra* manifestations of 'being,' viewers benefit from considering a future through processes of *becoming*. *Tu Mamá*'s youthful address makes the ever-becoming Real of the intersubjective shift possible—and manifest.

# 5 Maturity

Tenoch and Julio frequently appear immature, but this simple description and simple extrapolations to 'underdeveloped' nations like Mexico miss greater points. At about the same time as the great canon-building teenpics of the 1980s, leading scholarship on the genre of youth movies reproaches 'distorted' and simplistic treatments of youthfulness (Considine 1985: 9–11). David Considine argues that the best in the genre affords audiences 'a means by which we may view ourselves and our major social institutions':

> the images we see, the plots we encounter, the recurring themes and motifs that unfold, reflect not simply the views and values of the audience, not only the attitudes and ideas of the film creators, and not just the social conditions of the day, but an intricate and interwoven association of all these factors.
>
> (*ibid*: 11)

Consider *Sixteen Candles* (Hughes 1984). In spite of many merits, *Sixteen Candles* generically exemplifies a relatively stale conception of youthful identity in its conclusion. The film translates the ideal wedding in teen-hero terms. The resolution signaled at film's end by Molly Ringwald's Samantha in a ceremonial wedding (bridesmaid) dress leaning over her customary ('sweet sixteen' birthday) cake to ritualistically 'first kiss' dreamy Jake (Michael Shoeffling) fulfills the promises of her adolescence and assures her a future social-domestic arrangement (probably in Chicagoland). Samantha foregoes her (ritualistic birthday) wish because her (ritualistic adolescent-transition) wish has 'already come true.' Romance formulates her youthful identity and upper-middle-class conditions that surround it. Jake is assuredly Mr. Right, and viewers access this soft-focus romantically lit ideal not just maximally but implicitly, passively, and singularly through the transparent conventional narration and plot.

In the manner that youth movies and most narratives normally and normatively thrive on conflict leading to resolution, dissonance leading to consonance, imaging within the genre is indicative of our hope for personal transformations hand-in-hand with social-political concerns. The resolutions are satisfying in certain respects. *Sixteen Candles'* narrative patterns coalesce as a moral for youthful viewers. Much less often in youth films do the hurts leave noticeable impairment and scar; or, significant questions remain unanswered, largely unresolved around overlapping realities shaped as the very essence of adult existence. A teenage-lifespan away from Samantha's 'sweet sixteen,' they do just that in *Tu Mamá.*

First glance at the conversation Tenoch and Julio have after leaving the airport and merging into Mexico City's traffic, for example, suggests that political activism (and national identity and cultural citizenship), professional aspirations (and class and privilege), and potential love interests (based on sexual orientation, gender roles, heteronomativity, and more) are the highest stakes for the adolescent characters. And they are not terribly progressive on these scores, yet the themes make for enticing drama and for compelling, if isolated, interpretations of the film. By the time the sequence leaves viewers peering out the back window of the car at the corpse in the road, however, their readings either default to the singular themes or demand strategies to match the film's layers of complexity and alternating stylistic patterns.

By the 21st century the youth genre, claims Timothy Shary, evolves toward 'increasingly complex, dynamic' but also 'revealing depictions' of the transformational processes associated with youthfulness (2002: 209–10, 264). Further, according to Shary and Alexandra Seibel, as the genre overcomes the 'predominantly ethnocentric' stance of Hollywood and the classical style through independent and international cinemas, viewers gain a 'much greater diversity of experiences' (2007: 2–3). This amounts to nothing less than a 'shock' to the system (*ibid.*: 1).

On the one hand, the transitional and transformational processes of adolescence are 'natural,' universally 'familiar,' and

> filled with less spectacular phenomena, such as how we come to be accepted by society, discover romance, have sex, gain employment, make moral decisions, and learn about the world and who we are in it.
>
> (Shary 2002: 1–2)

On the other hand, the significance of symbols, tropes, ceremonies, and more distinctly rites of passage configure with generic aspects for insight to the social mechanisms they represent (Shary 2002: 226, 244; Lewis 1992: 63, 71, 82, 139).

Through much of *Tu Mamá,* adolescent passages are treated through vicariously embodied actions—standing in a hallway outside a doorway, crossing a threshold, neither here nor there but progressing through the world. The sense of community experienced through this liminal stance, usefully outlined in Victor Turner's landmark anthropological theories, enacts a poly-logical (dialogues, triads, etc.) 'dialectical process' between 'structure and anti-structure' for individuals and their communities (1969: 94–6, 131–5, 167). Rituals paradoxically convey tradition while also marking the arenas for potential social change and identity formulation; personal and interpersonal relationships can de-structure and transcend the norm-governed conventions and social mechanisms that hold them in place (*ibid.*: 97, 127–30).

Such a poststructural process interposes modes of 'humankindness' and egalitarian values against contrasting modes of 'status' with hierarchical values (*ibid.*: 97, 105). Yet it also reimagines these operations outside of strict binary terms: 'at a given moment many incumbencies of fixed positions coexist with many passages between positions' (*ibid.*). Mythologies of youth convey the liminal processes through tropes (like 'greetings' or corridors). Moreover, as 'life-crisis rites' engage ethical, existential, spiritual, and sacred meanings, the narratives elevate to the supernatural and fantastic: 'believers must pass on their way to the final and absolute states of heaven, nirvana, or utopia' where ultimately 'hierarchies are "inverted"' (*ibid.*: 195).

Ritualistic symbols and ceremonial actions associated with youthful mythologies offer useful comparisons for how genre studies consider adolescent identity formulation and processes of transformation. Shary makes a clarion call for an 'address' that offers 'a certain liberation for the natural development' associated with adolescence, especially 'youth sexuality' and similarly provocative, complex issues that are 'so often stunted by social codes,' which *Tu Mamá*'s youthful address answers (2002: 210).

Among the film's subjectivity, its youthful characters' focalized perspectives, and complex objective agencies, *Tu Mamá* gets away with revising generic patterns and proposing alternatives for a new global mainstream. Its narration appeases conventional tastes but redefines them for a 21st-century international audience. As for the comparison to *Sixteen Candles*, this means having our cake and deconstructing it too (and we can dismiss the analogy for *American Pie*).

*Tu Mamá* offers several ceremonial events as part of its depiction of adolescence, none more ritualistic than Tenoch's sister's wedding. The actual bride and groom receive little attention, whereas the ritualistic 'wedding' qualities are extrapolated to Julio and Tenoch 'meeting' Luisa. As the scene exposes and then disarms the social-status roles around the reception-party, the story emphasizes the reception/'receiving' and betrothal of our trio. Their engagement removes itself from traditional romance explicitly; instead, those values implicitly inform processes of youthful identity building. The film more than represents youthfulness and allegories dependent on immaturity; it xenochronically advances 'ways of reacting to' the complex, and sometimes ceremonially structured, transitions from youth to adulthood. In its complex forms, the film invites viewers into *experiences of becoming* through a precisely youthful address.

The wedding scene redresses continuity-style editing, as treated systematically throughout this film. It consists of 14 shots that create their own convoluted multitextural schemes and intermittent identifications, dialectically interchanging alignments alongside, sometimes momentarily through, and oftentimes against our characters. The first four shots average 2.5-second duration and comparably depict (most directly and dominantly) views of bodyguards/drivers for the elite guests of the wedding against a backdrop of the decorated venue, the Lienzo Charro del Pedregal in southern Mexico City. The ubiquity of armed guards speaks to states of security in this social condition as well as perhaps to conspicuous displays of power, especially politically contextualized authority, following such a high-ceremony event. That they are irreconcilably recognized as (merely) drivers (yet) with guns who serve their employers may lead viewers to interpret them fairly as multivalent symbols of larger hypocrisies and contradictions.

Contemporary defenses of political and economic social positions thematically coordinate with the current condition *writ large* as well as traditional notions of Mexican and Spanish-American culture. Less directly, *charro* riders appear as backdrop throughout the wedding sequence. *Charros* are 'horsemen.' As man and horse operate in tandem for their services, a bestial quality reflects back on the male-human rider. Unlike *vaqueros* or *rancheros*, *charros* are imbued with a Basque notion of 'crude' yet limitedly noble servitude. The word '*charro*' derives from Spanish-Basque '*txar*,' idiomatically 'poor or weak.' American vernacular historically connotes *charro* as a *mestizo-Mexicanidad* status above *indigeneity* but below New Spain.

Three lessons arise from the appearance of *charros* alongside driver/guards, food servers, and contemporarily placed workers: (1) people who most directly maintain the social condition are visible but ignored and denied its full access and privileges; (2) humanistic values are degraded accordingly but implicitly; and (3) this is not a new story but, as a matter of profundity, rather repeats in cycles through the ages built into customs and conventions and even costume. These stories repeat, yet their structures persist. As stories repeat, they invite reflection upon the structural determinations undergirding them.

Visually, each guard/driver shot and the four in symmetric, relatively rapid-fire succession offer structuralist-style collisions. Single medium-close-ups show a guard standing vertically while *charros* ride through the depth of the frame horizontally and forward or circle around behind with lassos twirling. Expressionistic and subtly oblique angles accentuate one another. Wedding decorations slice the frames, redefining spatio-temporal continuity and contextualizing social dynamics around the *lienzo* arena. The dominant visual anchor alternates right-left-right-left like a military march across these four shots [the first two illustrated in Figures 5.1 and 5.2]. In a rhythm of its own, and precisely against predominant rhythms of the shot-level visuals and cuts, Julio's voice-over counts aloud the number of guards he finds, like a child's pass-the-time game, '*seis-siete-ocho-nueve-diez-once, ¡pu-ta-mad-re!*' But counting 6-to-11-plus-expletive oddly strokes against

*Figure 5.1* 'Clashing' Images Depict Drivers/Guards, *Charros*, and *Lienzo* . . .

*Figure 5.2* . . . In Wedding Dramatic Re-enactments

the one-two-three-four visual beat of deep-focus one-shot guards. The effect is like listening to two songs at once, a military march like *Marcha Tierra Blanca* with jazz syncopation low in the background. The guards (ambivalently drivers) reify the social ranks of the wedding attendees for whom they work, even as the film's style destabilizes social mechanisms and resulting values. Clashes invite questions.

This scene's narrative throughline threads four long takes, between 16 and 45 seconds in duration each, all utilizing what is becoming familiar, a 'walking' hand-held camera that occasionally leans oblique. Viewership 'strolls' slightly aslant of the squared doorways, pillared passageways, and arched corridors that organize the Spanish Renaissance-informed, highly proportioned interiors. The long shots emphasize the paradoxically traditional-but-modern environment as much as or more than the situated characters themselves. Tenoch and Julio appear genuinely adolescent but 'out-of-place' in this (traditionally romantic) affair.

Tenoch as the bride's younger brother shares certain presumed familial obligations of greeting guests, including notably the nation's president in attendance; instead he hangs on the margins of the crowd with Julio and gets inebriated. Like at other events, Julio's invitation extends through Tenoch and is contingent upon their friendship and Tenoch's family's privilege. Tenoch's mother previously advised Julio he must 'look very sharp' because 'the president will be there.' Among other things, Julio's body language and mismatched, outdated suit with conspicuously ruffled shirt and cuffs show him off-step with the affluent, high-fashion partygoers. Julio's and Tenoch's behavior and appearance are low-scoring tests of maturity with standards established by their condition. Intermittent agency exorcises this determination and expands the lessons.

After Tenoch's father relieves him of his strong alcoholic drink, the objective camera hints at Julio's over-the-shoulder vantage but then denies his exit in favor of its own view of the *ruedo* center stage and reception activities. Then, at the bar, where Julio is rejected in his attempt to commiserate with the serving staff over the stuffy crowd ('what a bunch of assholes, right?'), the camera denies Julio's eyeline match as he discovers and watches Luisa. His view appropriates Luisa while she appears in frame, yet the negated eyeline match immobilizes his dehumanizing, misogynistic agency. The cross-rhythms complicate expectations of identification and focalization with 'main' characters and their presumed heroism. These suggest competing realities, which circulate the social space and are echoed by the adults. Tenoch's father declares the wedding's 'humble celebration' and emphasizes the president's 'great modesty' over his own daughter's bridal day, both of which are less than fully true. Julio and Tenoch believe themselves to be immune from the stifling political condition. Narration outsmarts their adolescent disillusionment.

The two longest takes in the wedding scene particularly stand out. The first, a 95-second shot, reveals Tenoch's conversation with his cousin, where polite small talk turns briskly to passive aggressive verbal jousting. Tenoch holds his own against Jano in one-upmanship; or, seeing it differently, Jano holds his own in arrested development. Alongside the competing aural-visual textures around depictions of this rivalry among cousins, Giménez Cacho's steadily bated voice-over, our seventh narrator entry growing familiar but thoroughgoingly tangential to the diegesis, backgrounds Jano's character with the 'discipline and technique' the elder cousin admonishes the younger for lacking. 'You have to create your own style,' professes Jano with both irony and dramatic irony, as he unwittingly dialogues with the heterodiegetic agencies and messages.

With the narrator's help, Jano reveals himself a man-boy, almost as adolescent as Tenoch but with some social niceties of his chronological age and fuller adoption of privileged upbringing. Under attack from Jano for his lack of worldly experience and inability to convey that in his creative writing, which he dreams of doing, Tenoch trades barbs, and the camera abets him by sliding right and slightly up to and behind his shoulder. The vaguely over-the-shoulder identification is relatively short-lived, however, and the long-take camera returns left and resets the quasi-objective stageline with Julio joining at center.

Julio sizes up Jano easily. Continuing the 95-second long take, now a three-shot, Julio kneels down in preparation of a trap on Jano, and the camera tilts down as temporary focalization with Julio and his caper. The trap springs, and Jano spills his wine on himself and erupts in a juvenile tantrum. As with any prank, timing is everything, and Jano's outburst fills the quieting reception in cadence with Tenoch's mom ringing out the start of the ceremonial father-of-the-bride toast. Given the subtle formal polyrhythms, the drama is deliberate but mostly understated compared to mainstream teenpics or even *Sólo con Tu Pareja* with its own ritualistic-romantic wedding party.

The humor and ironies fold on top of themselves, as Julio's dialogue first agrees mockingly with Jano's slight against Tenoch—'yeah, what do you know?'—but recasts the question subversively and rhetorically. The final piece of dialogue in this shot, performed low in volume and ignored entirely in the subtitling, may be lost from casual viewing but offers a prism by which other aspects of the shot refract into clearer meaning. Tenoch apologizes but with biting sarcasm. His apology to Jano, whispered but dagger sharp, '*fue sin querer*,' translates somewhat literally as 'it was not what I wanted' and idiomatically but passively (or passive aggressively) 'my mistake' (cf. Cuarón and Cuarón 2001: 89). This apology presents itself sarcastically and more conspicuously than a typical and conventionally applied '*disculpame*,' '*lo siento,*' or even the '*perdón*' offered at other story moments. This clause is also the title of Jano's recently published but critically panned book, which had been the ostensible basis of their warring conversation. Through the film's stylized language, thematic cues on youthfulness offer the viewer several layers of 'truth' and truth-building processes. Rather than anchor in teenage immaturity, the shifting address accumulates considerations of 'maturity' across competing realities to be sorted out.

A brief alternative reality of adult 'social order' at the bridal table depicts the ritualistic father-of-the-bride speech, which continues muted and off-screen. Backgrounds dialogue with foregrounds. Back across the *lienzo* arena, the scene's longest take serves as ceremonial climax of 'wedding'/'reception' functions. The shot is a deceptively simple, almost hypnotically ruminative 215-second long take of Julio and Tenoch meeting Luisa. Loosely, our three 'main' characters and the dynamics of their journey together are married, receive one another, but their exchange of vows stresses selfish interests rather than a blessed union.

Over the initial 36 seconds, Julio and Tenoch seek out, in youthfully superficial terms, 'the hot chick' and thrust themselves into meeting her. To draw a finer point, their macho-aggressive 'greeting her' converts the genial social-conventional act to emphatically objectify her; by contrast, a 'meeting with her' would have recognized her as a person and made possible greater intimacy in their mutual exchange. Luisa seems perplexed by their brusque approach. They remain oblivious. Perspective mixes subjective understandings with each character and objective assessment of them and the circumstances. Stylistic exigencies afford retrospection that interrogates the structural determinations of these actions and invites something different.

An inexplicably positioned camera seems to float in space outside the balcony rail where the three meet, slipping again slightly oblique. Julio and Tenoch advance from the right and corner Luisa dressed in elegant ivory satin against the black wrought-iron rail. Julio blurts out churlishly: 'is this boring or what?' The refined version of Luisa responds stiffly but demurely 'no'; easily she then divulges a more genuine answer that the wedding is 'a little' boring. At the top of the stair's landing, Tenoch and Julio aim to charm Luisa but demonstrate their adolescent self-centeredness and sense of entitlement as they block the passageway. Undaunted, Tenoch and Julio infer Luisa is Jano's wife as he arrives, and the voice-over narrator momentarily prioritizes her backstory.

Luisa lost her childhood. She was orphaned at age ten due to a car accident and pledged to take care of her infirm aunt. Rather than due to abandonment, divorce, or economic hardship as for Julio and Tenoch and as part of modern-mythic structures of adolescence, her parental absenteeism is by tragic design. Sacrifice suffuses her background. Her youthful backstory leaps to adult maturity before its time. Arguably more than she ever does with Tenoch or Julio, Luisa dotes on a childish Jano more as maternal figure than as spouse and equal partner. If Julio and Tenoch suggest adolescent parallels with modern Mexico, Luisa's becoming-adult story augments the allegorical associations through *Tu Mamá*'s mythologies of youth.

During their panicked action, she scrubs wine from Jano's blemished ivory linen suit, and the camera glides in, from long view to medium at closest, then back out in steady counter-melody. As Jano continues his puerile outbursts, first Luisa and then Tenoch join the crowd in polite hand-clapping applause (ostensibly for the *charros*). The majority of this 45-second middle segment of the 215-second shot demotes diegetic sound for the voice-over. As the narrator's eighth entry overrides Jano's juvenile hysterics in favor of Luisa's tale of sacrifice, the diegetic volume quiets. Clapping and crowd noises lightly punctuate the narrator's delivery and add textural counterpoints to the hypodiegetic information. Divided identifications further splinter among the present predicaments of the party and the past-to-future trajectories of Luisa's identity formation.

With Jano dispatched, Julio and Tenoch resume their charmless charms on Luisa [see Figure 5.3]. The remaining 134 seconds of this convoluted 215-second shot mimics the functions of classical-style continuity. A long view re-establishes Luisa at the rail on left where she started, but Julio and Tenoch stand and rejoin her. Through the kind of 'small world' coincidence that pleasantly often seems to bring people together for first meetings at social affairs like this, Tenoch confirms that she is Jano's wife and informs

*Figure 5.3* Ceremonies Surrounding Marriages, Weddings, and Reception

her that he is Jano's cousin. Luisa seems initially enthusiastic, even desperate, for any opportunity for friendly social engagement.

Luisa asks if he is the 'little Tenoch' she met years ago at a family gathering and then remarks that he is now 'quite the grown man.' Both are paradoxically and only partially true. Characters appear fragmentary. The address at this moment in the shot divides then multiplies our focalized identification with and empathy for ('little'/'grown man') Tenoch, (contingently invited/thoroughly ill-suited) Julio, and (greeted/objectified) Luisa. Equally, the vantage remains distant and precarious enough to interrogate the formative relationships and their occurrence in this highly ceremonial circumstance.

Julio's coarse bursts of laughter and then crooning 'woo' not only highlight his and Tenoch's adolescent awkwardness but stress the instability surrounding their in-formation maturity. Tenoch stands center and closer to Luisa, while Julio at far right dangles from another rail and literally climbs the wall like a fidgety child. Tenoch and Julio take turns at tests of maturity and mostly fail throughout this sequence. Both may be overly brash from strong drinks. Earlier Julio instructs Tenoch that pointing his finger is impolite but covertly 'adjusts' himself crudely in the same breath. Later Julio will cry out at the *mariachis* in applause that seems inappropriate for this exclusive crowd and ceremonious affair but expertly echoes classic '*mariachi grito.*' Is Julio an aberration, are the *mariachis* anachronisms, or are customs obsolete? The narrative skims past these and similar questions. Competing realities swirl in this social condition, shielded by ceremony and custom.

The clearest deficiency Tenoch and Julio display in this wedding scene comes through their unsophisticated propositioning of Luisa with a barely veiled invitation to visit the beach. Production Notes satirically highlight their behavior: they 'flirt with her with all the style and grace seventeen year-old boys are known for' (Anhelo 2002). Sensing opportunity, Julio hops in between Luisa and Tenoch, and the camera evenly glides in to a tighter view on the trio, though never closer than medium-size. Even as the three appear vertically near one another, graphically reinforced by poles and building features, the different character movements betray their varying social energies and maturity. With background temporarily limited, the camerawork can be read now as progressively subjective but potently conflicted—both allying with Julio's and Tenoch's predation and retreating with Luisa's avoidance. Agencies compete for attention.

Innuendo of fellatio lewdly overdetermines the destination, Boca del Cielo, 'Heaven's Mouth,' as innuendo of sex does the entire conversation. More, its divine descriptions as 'better than paradise' and 'a slice of heaven on earth' weigh against the material and exclusionary aspects of a little-known beach locale. Tenoch and Julio in fact do not know this location; they are fabricating this story/reality (partial truth or yet undiscovered idea) as an adolescent fantasy. Auspicious glances between Julio and Tenoch throughout this wedding scene suggest they somehow see past the adult-world pretenses and materialist elitism, perhaps even arrogantly stand above the corruption that has purchased much of it.

Among other things chauvinistic, their fantasy hypocritically redraws similar exclusionary politics, just further toward their advantage and in late-1990s-*Chilango*-teen terms of avoiding 'yuppie backpackers and wanna-be surfers' and knowing what only the 'locals' know. They wish to serve as gatekeepers in this fantasy and recreate the environmental conditions for what they imagine as their needs—sex, beer, and a perfect combination of lazing about and adventurous experience. Immediately more hedonistic than existential, these needs have virtue as authentically teenage idealizations. Equally they project those idealizations mistakenly onto Luisa. Julio and Tenoch ignore the reality that respectfully actualizes Luisa in favor of their reimagined one. Yet, stylistic dynamics afford careful retrospection. The film's youthful address dismantles this Imaginary, narrating the multiple realities that coexist for and around our characters and revealing the values alongside their prescriptive codes.

The desirous tensions play out with the camera inching tighter on our characters and surrounding sounds barely audible. Julio and Tenoch seem to feed off of each other's pubescent energy, growing louder and more boisterous. They objectify Luisa in the fantasy to the point of overlooking her 'person' while approximating her body until Julio magnanimously offers in the third-person 'she should come along.' Luisa occasionally scans the wedding crowd, like looking for a reason to excuse herself—even hopping the rail for any escape. Finally, gracefully (unlike Ceci or Ana), she informs them that she is not available for their adolescent fantasy, which contravenes the encroachment of the camera. She momentarily redirects both the storyworld and the camera to the *mariachis* taking center stage. Radical reflection peels layers of socially structured values away from the significance of these events and offers opportunities for reformulation. The vying for romantic power, not just socially but ceremonially inscripted, parallels the exchanges of agency between Luisa and the adolescents. The alternating stylistic impulses within this long-take shot and its sequential placement formulate *Tu Mamá*'s conceptual continuity. Never overriding story elements and thematic concerns, the film offers looks into and through the experiential processes of characters' in-formation identities.

The *denouement* of the wedding scene again redirects the agency and our identifications. A female food server strides from guest spaces, to then 'servant quarters' kitchen space, to finally the parking lot where driver/ guards are fed. Cuts across the four shots of this scene-level conclusion are paradoxically both hidden and accentuated by the pillars and doorways the server crosses. Cinematic form showcases the building's fenestrations and the environmental architecture that both hold the social values in place and hold them up for our examination.

For hero-driven expectations of the narrative, this miniature story may seem extraneous or supplementary—a 'digression' or possible 'little dissertation' in classical-style conceptions (Bordwell 1985: 52–3). And the voice-over narration, the film's ninth entry, which also bridges into the following scene, further complicates formal matters.

Diegetic mariachi music starts full volume, then abruptly filters through point-of-audition with our new 'minor' character, food server with tray, for almost 2 seconds; then diegetic sound silences entirely for almost 2 seconds before the narrator acousmatically enters.

Parts of this scene's voice-over narration, as entries do elsewhere too, reach relatively far afield of the story's 'major' and even 'minor' characters to comment on seeming non sequiturs, but these may also serve as semi-logical associations among coexisting partial truths that are too often ignored. Backgrounds strangely refocus foregrounds. Here, for example, viewers learn among other things: (1) the irony of the president's 'busy schedule' while he sits idle and lower-class servers work diligently; (2) the injustice that guards, chauffeurs, *mariachis*, and *charros* actually do work in this moment without full credit, honor, or benefit and have for ages; (3) the hypocrisy of the president's comments on the Cerro Verde massacre and condolences for victims' families against his administrative support of state government and neoliberal global capitalism. Though a brief interlude, its multiple textures highlight for viewers qualitatively significant and unforeseen opportunities for identification across Mexico's diverse cultural makeup and its coexisting but irreconcilable realities. Questions nevertheless outnumber the answers.

The wedding reception delineates its own mini-narrative structure and, especially through ceremony, revises generic features. The reception scene further operates amid a complex five-part chain of events:

1.  Tenoch's and Julio's first visit to the country club pool and shower together;
2.  the wedding reception;
3.  Luisa's visit to the physician;
4.  Tenoch's and Julio's second visit to the country club;
5.  and, Luisa with medical results receiving Jano's drunken confession by long-distance phone call.

The story initially seems fairly linear. Two events primarily depict the 'routine' of the adolescents' immaturity, and two initiate a process of change for and through Luisa. The party scene's ceremonial quality, upon radical reflection, acts as a gravitational force holding these events in a constellation.

In the first country club visit and the wedding scene, Julio's and Tenoch's immaturity is fully on display. Both reflect the film's conceptual continuity, where the country club setting situates them ambiguously among class-institutional values and the wedding confirms them through tradition and ceremony. This series of actions then leads to Luisa's visit to the physician's office. A long take protracts the stylistic patterns of the on-going sequence. The voice-over narrator bridges the scenes with a simple semantic transition that 'days passed.' Even casual viewers surely pause, unsure about this segue. Luisa takes a pop-psychology quiz entitled 'Are You a Fully Realized Woman?' Luisa's scores indicate she prefers 'to be awake rather than sleeping or dreaming'; values 'time more highly than money or power'; and thinks 'more about the present than the past or the future.' As multiple-choice options, these binary answers can be nothing but partial truths, partial insights to her character, disguised as (pseudo)science.

Contrasting the soundtrack textures, the 46-second hand-held shot begins with a high-angle full view on Luisa sitting in the waiting room and walks back anticipatory of her eye-level meeting the nurse and doctor. Her quiz score reductively summarizes, not entirely unlike juvenile appropriations of her at the wedding, her as 'a woman afraid to claim her freedom.' The narrator discloses: 'Luisa didn't agree.' Like the three-part chiasmus of these 'self' assessments, she crosses three thresholds, from waiting room to nurse station to office with a blue door, which the doctor closes. The door image as well as its shutting sound in low-volume under the hypodiegetic narrator counter-rhythmically predict the cut. The tropes exceed cinematic puns as part of the narrational system.

From this long take the next link in the sequential chain is a six-shot scene with Tenoch and Julio back at the country club pool masturbating together on the diving boards. First-time viewers surely wonder where this story is going. Some will be distracted and alerted, comparable to the film's opening, by this semi-public act of indecency. The six shots follow inside-out editing patterns but with expressionistic angles on the characters. A rite of passage perhaps, a frank quality of sharing of intimacy accompanies this orgiastic experience. Imaginary group sex, this action likely seems initially salacious, not too far away from the proverbial 'letter to *Penthouse*.' But across this stylized sequential chain, the unique logic of its youthful address emphasizes their exchange of desires and agencies toward explorations of in-formation identities.

The subtly unconventional aesthetics and conceptual-continuity editing of this second country club scene strike a discord with the last link across this exemplary sequential chain but adds to the strange dialectics. A 122-second long take reveals Luisa alone in the privacy of her bedroom [see Figure 5.4]. A full shot reveals her in undergarments that are more utilitarian than

*Figure 5.4* Forsaken Luisa

alluring, but with intimate disclosure nonetheless. In misdirection to the initial higher angle on her in the physician's waiting room, a low angle reveals Luisa lying atop the bed covers. Over the opening 12 seconds, Luisa stares intently down her body and toward a nondescript manila envelope by her side, and then lulls with arms crossed over her chest, head resting on her far shoulder, and eyes closed. Viewers focalize with her examining the envelope and then hang with the unanswered question as she lies inactive. Propped up by pillows at the headboard, her repose recalls sacrificial images of Christ on the crucifix. Her miniature death moment puns with but xenochronically juxtaposes the immediately preceding images of *les petits morts* from juvenile masturbation by Tenoch and Julio, the latter even grunting *'la Ess-pañola'* as his make-believe climactic object. Her enduring long-take presence and subjective agency in this bedroom contrast with her ethereal entity across continuity shots at the country club.

Over the next minute of this long take, she will answer the drunken call from Jano, still away at his summer symposium. Jano prioritizes his self-centered interests while Luisa continues the drudgery of getting them both settled after intercontinental relocation. Sacrifice permeates her. Although mostly stationery, but never perfectly steady, the hand-held shot leans forward over the next 64 seconds and embodies Luisa's growing courage to share something with Jano. His drunkenness prevents him from being available for her, his marital partner, and the focalized intensity with Luisa wanes. Where the voice-over at the wedding overturned Jano's juvenile outburst in favor of Luisa's backstory, here Jano's voice-over-phone dominates Luisa and her needs. Jano's selfishness, not unlike Julio's and Tenoch's regularly, converts the conversation on separate tracks to a one-sided, one-dimensional confession that he has been unfaithful again. Luisa is multiply, manifoldly forsaken. Leaning back in some resignation, over the next 35 seconds of the long take Luisa repeatedly poses her emotional state as rhetorical question: 'why are you telling me this?' She weeps passionately. For the final 11 seconds of the shot, the camera collapses with Luisa across the bed with the crumpled envelope still to her side.

Among the partial truths from Luisa across this long take, viewers may doubt the value of her numerous sacrifices and wonder if she is indeed a woman able 'to claim her freedom' as she believes but is unable to test true. Her adult identity appears in-crisis. Even first-time viewers begin to ascertain that the envelope at her side has some significance and probably in relation to her physician's appointment in sequential chain. Reflection upon the conceptual continuity advances associations greater than linear-causal effects, even if they are not entirely resolved. Across this sequential chain, Luisa's existentialism does not negate but thoroughly recasts even the most sophomoric concerns and identity questioning for Julio and Tenoch, particularly as they begin their journey together.

The sequence continues beyond these five links, to be sure. Certainly similar sequential chains assemble throughout the film, several anchored by mythic experiences of growth. From considerations of maturity, especially those scripted around ceremonies and rituals and according to youth genre aspects, *Tu Mamá*'s treatments of sexuality warrant particularly careful attention.

# 6  Sex

How 'sexy' is the sexuality in *Tu Mamá* really? Contemporary reception and reviews almost without exception blow the issue out of proportion, and most critical assessments follow suit in misreading sexual themes. North American home-market packaging advantaged this idea by citing popular press descriptions—'unafraid of sexuality,' 'without doubt the sexiest film you'll see this year,' and 'wildly erotic!' U.K. DVD marketing summarizes the story as 'a steamy, sexy, and sun-drenched sensation,' and Spanish packaging romantically aligns 'freedom, innocence, and sex.' Presumed sexiness has been part of the film's interest since it was released.

Leonardo García Tsao's review goes as far as to describe the sexual fantasy as something 'straight out of *Penthouse*' and the male characters as 'underdeveloped' like 'oversexed' Beavis and Butt-Head (2001: 24). Pat Aufderheide's reading echoes the point initially, emphasizing a *Dumb and Dumber*-type 'tone of adolescent taunt' suggested in the film's title and sexuality comparably described as 'sexy,' 'dirty,' and 'raunchy' (2001: 32–3). Aufderheide carefully complicates her assessment by acknowledging its 'self-reflexive narrative' operating in several ways (*ibid.*). I highlight these two reviews not to disparage their characterizations but because, precisely from two of the keenest critical voices in Latin American media studies, their readings are potent and symptomatic. It is difficult to find critical reception that does not at least mention *Tu Mamá*'s presumed sexiness.

Part of the challenge of this film is its intricacies of tone across narrative levels, which render several isolated and possibly contradictory interpretations accurate and even compelling. Each isolated reading delivers '*una verdad incompleta*,' just one more partial truth in a series of partial truths, as explained by the narrator. The partial truths revolve around our characters' lives, especially their sexually mature identities, in individual ways and for existential-type questions but also extrapolate to larger issues. For this film, viewers would be advised to not become engrossed in any one partial truth but instead step back to see how the parts figure together before reaching for specifics. It is not by coincidence that our hand-held long takes frequently do exactly this in vicariously embodied movement and visual scope: take in the long view before 'walking' into the action and never so close to absorb so fully into one character and idea as to forget the intricate network of contexts surrounding them. In fact, there are fewer than a handful of shots throughout this entire film that would be defined easily as closer than a medium view and these mostly for detail on action. Sexuality can lure viewers into doing this though, closing in on the intensity of the sexual act, but *Tu Mamá* demands equal attention across these story parts and their partial truths.

The partial truths aggregate into a social condition these characters live in and struggle against. Traditional conceptions of sexuality tend to hold these structures in place, whereas reinventions of sexuality offer the possibility for change, the possibilities of revolution. The admittedly crude and unorthodox behavior of the characters must be read as such but also as just one part of the film's complicated textures. Paul Julian Smith (after noting the 'smart and sexy' aspects of *Tu Mamá*) frames this idea with respect to tone perfectly, that 'to accuse the film of crudeness is not only to misread its grungy technique but to confuse the characters' viewpoints with the film's own' (2002: 16–17). Each part demands close reading itself but then again as a component of a sequential chain of xenochronically 'strange' combinations; this is as true for the tones mixing across the film with comparable thematic devices as it is for the narrative events that depict sexuality.

The funny thing is, *Tu Mamá*'s treatments of sexuality are not very 'sexy' at all. That is, as the director repeatedly explains, most of the sex in this film is 'awkward,' 'clumsy,' 'really brief and bad,' which is 'what teen sex is like': 'we weren't trying to create steamy sex scenes' but instead were hoping to capture a 'moment of honesty' (quoted in Basoli 2002: 28; Lawrenson 2002: 19). Multiple viewings and reflective readings prove this. *Tu Mamá*'s sex scenes, when not censored, refute the hypocritical moralizing and repression that encompasses mainstream treatments of adolescence, especially in the style of *American Pie* and its youth movie ilk, according to the filmmakers (Lawrenson 2002: 19). The acts of questioning and development that involve sexual identity offer remedies for the failings of 'normal' youth films.

Censorship, in the director's own transactional but tongue-in-cheek phrasing, 'castrated' the film (quoted in Hirschberg 2003). But what gets 'castrated,' excised of its own material potency and symbolic powers, is not a set of steamy sex scenes but rather the opportunity to explore intimacy and discover mutual respect and empathic understanding among the characters in their millennial social condition. The censored version jeopardizes rich opportunities for identification the uncensored film provides. Its moments of honesty transcend 'truer' depictions of youthful sex and return the hermeneutics to originary signification and primordial considerations of identity building experiences. The ritualistic passages of adolescence and the widely applicable but multifaceted youthful address of this film concentrate the action and meaning of these potential growths. The key is recognizing that sexuality is far less about sex and far more about questioning values of intimacy.

Reconsider *Tu Mamá*'s opening images. At the beginning and end of the uncensored opening shot, the hand-held camera 'looks' then 'walks' into and back out of the doorway of Ana's bedroom, her adolescent-specific private space. The formal effect of this long-take walking shot impersonates the outside-in editing pattern of classical style, yet its establishing view commingles objective and subjective stances. With rack focusing from interior-long to full, the continuous shot never gets closer to one of the pair nor privileges identification with one character more than the other in ways that shot-countershot conventions normally do—and do all the more thoroughly with close-up shots. Tenoch appears initially on top and in some manner of control, but after having reached orgasm and appearing spent he buries his face in the mattress, which is where the R-rated plot merely begins.

In addition to the very first 20 seconds, as stated earlier, the R-rated text also excises the final 23 seconds, rendering the opening shot 78 seconds in total duration with significant alterations to the soundtrack as well. Still reasonably considered a long take aesthetically, the excised portions are significant. With the initial 20 seconds of clumsy, impatient, self-serving teenage sex dramatically depicted, this post-coital embrace appears less thoroughgoingly 'coital,' literally a 'coming-together' moment that, Ana would surely attest, remains utterly unfulfilled. The Cuaróns' script decodes her reaction: 'loving and complicit, she fakes her orgasm' (2001: 61).

Tenoch's body lies parallel to the top one-third of the frame, while Ana's body crosses against his, a subtle visual collision that reflects their misalignments in sexual union and emotional maturity. Ana caresses and kisses Tenoch's forearm, a gesture that at once reads tender but, given the lack of affectionate body and eye contact between them as well as the rapidity of his climax compared to the deferment of hers, also consolatory. As she does this, Tenoch begins interrogating her about remaining faithful to him while she travels in Europe.

He frames his entitled expectations in self-centered commands to Ana, 'you promise to me' that you will not cheat. Tenoch conflates the sexual-romantic pact with hate-filled jingoistic slurs for the people with whom he fears she will have sex—'gringo backpackers,' 'French fags,' and 'any of those dirty Mexicans selling bracelets on the Riviera.' If viewers and reception reviews seem awestruck by the apparent sexiness and graphic corporeal disclosures, they should be at least equally appalled by the conceit and entitlement in Tenoch's voice. The last affront surely incited reactions among audiences during its domestic theatrical release. Sexuality and political sensibilities coalesce in a framework of adolescent immaturity. Cinematography punctuates this by the hand-held high angle lowering to an eye-level that finally sets a stageline for this scene.

While in constant hand-held motion throughout this opening scene, the camera steadies for the negotiations between the teen lovers. Ana's reaction to Tenoch's demands follows a fairly reasonable course from surprise at the accusation to consoling his insecurity. With a subtle lift of the hand-held camera, in the grammar of a cut, the long-take full shot subtly resets the scene as Ana literally flips the situation in a wrestling maneuver. The single take holds these affiliated ideas in a fluid motion. The power dynamic is synergistic.

With Ana now on top, her loving complicity slips into sarcastic teasing of Tenoch's fragile ego. Tenoch tries to push her aside and release himself, so she pins him down and turns the tables, '¿*y tu?*,' and 'what about you?' Physically overpowering him, she insists on her equal part in this negotiation. Her suggestion toward a compassionate, reciprocal sense of their bond erases; her patience runs thin; and she reinstitutes a power-over relationship, just with her now on top.

Behind the light-hearted joking between the pair, an implicit cultural and political chauvinism enlists the litany of the national characters, largely improvised by the actors during the shoot, with whom the teens promise not to make love (*ibid.*: 114 n1). The characters seem to culturally agree on these things. How seriously can these teenage promises of fidelity be taken? Ana ends with '*y tu padre*,' 'and your father,' which revises the gendered taunt in the film's title and takes a poke viewers cannot fully feel until the end of the film. Nudity in this scene, far from sensationalistic, reflects disclosures, if not fully genuine, effective, nor honorable, in the attempt by adolescents to manage their relationship with emotional maturity. Rite-of-passage sexuality tests their limits and abilities as mature individuals.

The unrated version of the film tracks back out of Ana's bedroom door and cuts to the thematically matching scene with Julio's goodbye to his girlfriend Ceci at her parent's house. The first instance of the film's voice-over narration bridges these scenes, entering just after an off-screen siren wail reminds viewers of the world's dangers just outside these safe, enriched family homes. The characters do not seem affected by the siren, but the alert should be tactfully abundant to viewers. The narration, hovering omnisciently among the diegetic information but apart from it, explains that Ana's mother, a French divorcee, 'didn't object to Tenoch,' referring directly to his romantic-sexual relationship with her daughter, but 'for Julio it was different.'

'Different' must be read xenochronic-dialectically here—and elsewhere. That 'it was *different*' rings true for character differences, especially as they are sketched out this early in the film and elucidated in the screenplay (*ibid.*: 9–57) The hint of parental judgment in favor of Tenoch and against Julio as romantic pairings for their daughters leaves unsaid comparable judgements over economic class, political clout, and presumed cultural sophistication. But also more significantly different are the stylistic pattern and narrational strategies by which viewers gather information about these two characters across these first two scenes. From the first scene's long single take to the second scene's multiplex of continuity-based editing with its own integrated long take, the alternating stylistic system introduces the youthful characters differentially amid their conditioning environments. The voice-over and long-take techniques carry information in a threshold space above and alongside but related to what viewers gather from the diegesis. The youthful address consolidates these as 'wild' insights to identity transformation.

Ceci's parents as adults hold in place several parental and marital stereotypes, as does the space of the home some traditional Mexican social conditions. Her mother, a 'Lacanian psychologist,' meta-textually and ironically overlooks all the signs and believes that the teens' relationship is 'innocent,' but her father, a pediatrician, believes that their relationship 'would go too far.' Here, the narrator agency's omniscience not only reveals knowingness across the full reach of the characters but also travels time and into the subjunctive-hypothetical. In proposing what 'would' happen, it invites viewers to interrogate more broadly than mainstream films typically do but in a fairly tactful, attainable manner. By contrast, in the storyworld several 'knowing' glances between the men betray a macho conception of the mother and daughter being scattered and impractical, and the father also rudely refuses to lower his newspaper and engage Julio in respectful social engagement. The wife browbeats all other family members in order to assert her opinion or instruction.

Accusing the film of stereotyping at this point again confuses characters' viewpoints with the film's own (Smith 2002). These adults are emotionally immature in their own ways, and Julio's character gets lost in power dynamics. Viewers initially access the scene from character level, especially empathetic with Julio's sense of displacement; yet at the same time, the counter-textural voice-over narration affords a subtly self-conscious view on youthfulness and how Julio's is figured through his romantic relationship with Ceci. The continuity-based treatments in this scene, opposed to the previous opening long-take shot most emphatically encapsulate Julio and his in-formation identity. The scene hints at conventionality but deserves review and inspection.

The scene lasts roughly 1:46, with three shots totaling 50 seconds downstairs and six shots totaling 56 seconds upstairs in Ceci's bedroom. The first downstairs shot models the hand-held 'walking' shot from the film's opening but in long take that lasts roughly only 10 seconds. It is worth noting that, according to the Cuaróns' screenplay notes, the first cut of this film included the tried-and-true exterior view of the family home before cutting to interior shots, but the filmmakers removed it at the advice of Guillermo del Toro and in their aim to adhere to but nuance conventional aspects (2001: 114 n3). At the start of this shot, a vantage from a foyer looks into a well-lit living room, but the abundance of upper-middle-class furnishings as well as a mirror reflection of them fill two-thirds of the frame from right and obscures a high-angle view onto a seated Julio whose back is to the camera [see Figure 6.1]. This view reminiscently rhymes with the opening shot looking past the corridor and Ana's bedroom door. Cuts following the first shot of this scene tend to invoke continuity-editing patterns, but they do so to highlight Julio, dressed in grey, blending in with the also grey couch upholstery and ivory-and-grey affluent surroundings. All is fairly bourgeois bland. He shields himself with a throw pillow, similarly grey, and meekly sips from a prim juice glass. His awkwardness and discomfort are apparent even before his call to perform sexually.

As a ruse, Ceci beckons him upstairs to help her retrieve her passport, but before heading upstairs Julio looks to Ceci's mother for permission. Obeying commands and stepping lightly, Julio's body language reflects his lower station and economic class all the more conscripted by these bourgeoisie surroundings. Continuity-based form holds these values in place as well. Once upstairs, Ceci propositions him but does so through verbally abusive commands and crude insults, which are structured by a fairly quick

*Figure 6.1* Different but Similar, Difficult Commencements—Julio Awaiting Admittance

shot-countershot exchange. Untranslated in the English subtitles, Ceci calls Julio '*bicho*,' which is merely demeaning if first translated as 'insect' but carries even more gendered synecdochal and imbruting notions when heard in *Chilango* slang as 'penis' or 'prick.' Julio acquiesces.

Interestingly, pictures of Julio hang on the wall among the somewhat stereotypical trappings one would expect in the teenage girl's bedroom [see Figure 6.2]. As Julio accepts the sexual proposition, the framed pictures appear behind him as backdrop for this rendezvous. The still images show him with hands covering parts of his face in various contortions. At once this is a playful game of teenage peek-a-boo held frozen in time for Ceci's amusement and room decoration, but it also spatially fulfills the negation of Julio's in-formation identity in this ideologically weighted 'intimate' circumstance. Her bedroom space and the domestic arrangement of the family home constrict Julio, and, complicit, he fails not just to escape but to recognize his confinement.

The adolescents engage in sexual intercourse, a Ceci-mandated 'quickie.' This teen sex does not enjoy a burst of spontaneous emotional connectedness but instead emphasizes desperation, impatience, and emotional indifference. There is no foreplay nor arousal. If Ana at least initially consoles Tenoch, Ceci derides Julio's anxious manhood throughout. A slight giggle and bubbly '*sí*,' 'yeah,' from her both confirms Julio's insertion and undercuts its 'macho-masculine' impact. Ceci initiates conversation during intercourse that removes the union from any emotional exchange and also replays some

*Figure 6.2* Gabriel García Márquez Portrait Meets Baby Seal Poster Meets Old and New Cameras—Backgrounds for an Unwitting Julio Crossing Thresholds

of Tenoch's uncertainty and accusatory nature. 'Tell me, will you go out tonight?,' she commands Julio to answer, to which he lies 'no way, baby,' and explains that he will be 'too lonely' missing her to go out. Their love-making and conversation are rote at best, and due to interruption neither climaxes. It is figuratively unconsummated.

A 47-second long take captures this consummating-unconsummated part of the scene, catalogued within the shot-countershot around it. This long-take view of Julio and Ceci mimics the conjugal relationship downstairs. Rather than just observing neatly and objectively, this long take extends the range of subjective and objective information viewers anticipate according to classical style. As with the previous teen-sex scene, there are paradoxical suggestions both for the characters and for viewers of inclusion-exclusion and enticement-observation. Positioned so firmly by his condition and the power dynamics of the family he is visiting, Julio's unequivocal answer ('no way, baby') defies what he knows and hopes to be true. Any possibility for meaningful, intimate exchange between Julio and Ceci is canceled.

In his discussions of modern 'transformations of intimacy,' Anthony Giddens revises late-20th-century understandings of sexuality. He draws parallels between narratives of self-identity, specifically through centuries-old literary romance, and contemporaneous conceptions of 'romantic love' (1992: 39–40). Both are formulaic and over centuries align with conventional views and ceremonial acts of love and sexuality (*ibid.*: 40). By the 20th century, this traditional concept of romantic love holds in place private and personal notions of an individual's relationship to sexuality as well as pressures of repression (shame, guilt, etc.) from norms and social institutions. Giddens explains that procreation, male-female binary conceptions of gender, and resulting romantic roles reinforce these traditional conceptions of romance, love, sex, and identity, and vice versa (*ibid.*: 61–4). Out of modern feminist conceptions of individual autonomy and sexual pleasure divorced from demands of biological reproduction, Giddens proposes that a 'plastic sexuality' decenters the traditional model and feeds our broadly conceived 'sexual revolution' beginning in the last decades of the 20th century (*ibid.*: 2–3).

Millennial-revolutionary realignments not only allow a different interpretation of the ideal values situated within 'romantic love' but also permutate the structure by which we define love as 'confluent,' one based on mutual exchange and reciprocity. Notice also that romantic and confluent love as dichotomous concepts (and Giddens' theoretical gestures to get there) offer certain parallels to *Tu Mamá*'s range of (post)structural qualities and influences. As a framework (and reframing alongside xenochronic anamorphosis), sexuality de-structures romantic love's notions of monogamy, fidelity, and finding the 'special person' in differential conversion to confluent love's purer 'special relationship' that is relationally contingent. Sex serves as part of confluent love's shared 'emotional order' guided by an 'exploration of the potentialities . . . of equality and mutuality' (*ibid.*: 61, 2).

*Tu Mamá*'s mythologies of youth revolve around not just mundane dramas but such explorations and tests of a mutually respectful emotional order. Most are low-scoring or failed tests comparable to the real trial-and-error of adolescence. And Julio and Tenoch are not overachievers nor precocious by most estimations. Luisa bests them. The film fortunately exceeds all their limitations. Networks sketch an outline around them. In fairly explicit ways as well as a number of implicit and figurative ways, sex serves the film's processes toward transformations of intimacy.

The film is effectively riddled with treatments of adolescent sex, intergenerational sex, group sex, and masturbation, some of it fully heterosexual and potentially heteronormatively grounded by Mexican and Western-world traditions and some of it blurring lines around conventionally defined heterosexuality, homosociality, homoeroticism, and homosexuality. Much is embodied, while some is imaginary. Particularly as correlated acts of nudity, voyeurism, and more general instances of 'indiscretion' are added in, distinctions of public and private spaces get blurred and redrawn as well.

Seemingly asexual topics and actions engage as much as explicitly sexual ones do our questions of intimacy. While a spectrum at least from straight through LGBTQ considerations lends itself to isolated readings of sexual-political identities at stake in *Tu Mamá*, the larger pattern leaves us with a Q+ of 'questioning' all of these and their overlapping contexts. The Cuarón brand of cinema language facilitates these overlaps. The film's conceptual continuity accentuates combinations of particular narrative events in sequences and in rhyming patterns across the film. Each sex act can be read in isolation according to its situation in the narration and storyline, and probably should be for its own political messages. And yet, through strange associations, a network around sexuality reveals its own structural determinations and affords a broader range of millennial transformations of intimacy.

After first seeing Tenoch and Julio sexually engaged with their girlfriends as discussed earlier, viewers encounter a more gradual disclosure of their various sex-related and erotic interests. They agree at the airport that this 'good-bye bullshit' is 'too much.' This shared honesty stands in some contrast not only to their sexual engagements and conversations with their girlfriends that same morning and the night before but also to their clichéd 'I'll miss you so much' statements at face and in somewhat 'synchronous' relationship to one another. Put more bluntly, in this singular time and place, Julio and Tenoch admit one thing but think and feel another. They lack the courage to be honest about these differences.

Julio's and Tenoch's hypocrisy and deceit are echoed by what their girl-friends say to them before departing for Italy—'I don't want to go'—as opposed to what they share privately to one another—'I want to be there already.' This scene is treated as a 70-second hand-held long take that hovers in and out of the characters' subjectivity alongside our second voice-over entry. The narrator states that Ana's father refers to Tenoch as 'the prep-pie' with his colleagues but 'never in front of his daughter.' Adults betray their own immaturity over sharing intimate information. The convoluted narration reveals not just lies, nor just hypocritical and contradictory statements, but countervailing realities for these 'major' and 'minor' characters and their incompatible living conditions that necessarily coexist in this time and space. Although these airport conversations do not immediately present themselves as 'sexual'—and certainly not 'sexy' and 'steamy'—they betray the sex-related forms of intimacy at stake throughout the film's journey.

As a further gradual disclosure in the car leaving the airport, a debate over the relative merits of economics, professional aspirations, Zapatista demonstrations, and contemporary urban existence seems to simply resolve itself in teen-sexual terms. Tenoch and Julio agree that 'left-wing chicks are hot, dude'—and after a beat of sexual fantasizing overriding any other thought, 'totally!' Casual viewers might be distracted by the strikingly adolescent tone of the debate, two characters literally 'farting around' and then joking that it smells like '*pan*,' 'bread,' but with a pun on the political party PAN. A few viewers might lend themselves to the characters' perspectives and get caught fantasizing themselves. The film makes a joke out of this by showing Julio and Tenoch occasionally brush one another's eyelids hypnotically before snapping fingers to 'reawaken.' The filmmakers demonstrate these young characters are 'controlled by their hormones' (Anhelo 2002). The response 'totally' at once punctuates the sexist point, as Alfonso Cuarón suggested, 'when you're a teenager, sex is the only thing you have in your head . . . getting laid is like an image of Disneyland, all magic and happiness' (quoted in Lawrenson 2002: 19). Yet, as the director emphasizes, sex in *Tu Mamá* dispels these romantically fantastic images and tries 'to create a moment of honesty' (quoted in *ibid.*). The 'moment of honesty' lies not in solely 'truer' representations but in exposing their operations and assumptions.

The simplicity of Tenoch's and Julio's debate and its conclusion in 'hot chicks' sanctioned through adolescent subjectivity underlies a deeper honesty through less explicit punctuation in the subtly unconventional shot-countershot that depicts the conversation. The scene depicts Julio and Tenoch slightly off-center in turns then resets along a stageline obliquely across the front windshield outside the car looking in. Preceding this, a bridging, functionally conventional establishing shot [see Figure 6.3] reveals their car pulling away from the curb at the airport, merging into left-to-right traffic in convergence with the infrastructure of Mexico City but in

*Figure 6.3* Traffic Collisions, Clashes With Infrastructure

graphic collision with a plane (Ana's and Ceci's plane?) seconds after take-off flying low overhead right-to-left and lifting away. Inclined toward classical paradigm readings, viewers likely find themselves caught in-between agencies in and around the characters and their travel with multiple access points to the information in this scene—not so striking as to appear illegible but striking enough to prepare a more complicated reading to follow.

Over the last 2.5 seconds of the shot-countershot, diegetic sound silences and the third voice-over narration redirects our interests to a more serious but largely ignored debate around everyday-tragic stories of the metropolis. The camera's sublime view coordinates with voice-over technique. Namely, narration indicates the benefit of social activism through public demonstrations and the avoidable death of Marcelino Escutia, the migrant bricklayer killed due to the same city infrastructure that Tenoch and Julio find themselves stuck in, frustrated by, complaining about, but still merging into.

The final shot of this scene initially enacts an over-the-driver's-shoulder view of the roadside crime scene, imitating Tenoch's focalized recognition of the death. There is actually little to gather from particularly his reaction. But this 28-second long take pans after about 8 seconds from over-the-shoulder angle to about 6 seconds of suggested subjectivity imagined through a diegetically nonexistent backseat passenger tangential to the characters' realm and finally shifts for the remaining 14 seconds to a de-subjectified yet quasi-embodied view out the back windshield [see Figure 6.4]. *Tu Mamá*'s address emulates the very process of trying to overcome myopia. The shot divides interests among the film's stories and enters the points of debate from relatively very different positions. It intimates then resists

*Figure 6.4* Retrospective Commemoration of Marcelino Escutia, Deceased Migrant
      Bricklayer

classical paradigm readings through embodied retrospection. For this length
of time, even only about 14 seconds, viewers ponder the importance of this
'minor' deceased character and the conditions surrounding his mortal life.
Perhaps we should appreciate characters and their stories regardless of traditional 'major' and 'minor' distinctions just as many of us hope for greater
equality outside the film and theatre. As the scene's action 'drives forward,'
characters' in-formation identities and values attached to them are exposed
for reflection.

These ideas present a strange combination to be sure, and all the more
as scenes link with scenes across Act One sequences. Although sexuality is
merely mentioned by the adolescent characters here, the larger transformations of intimacy formulate the more profound issues at stake in this scene.
How much do these two adolescent characters care about one another, about
their potential sexual partners ('hot chicks' and otherwise), about their fel-
low national-global citizens and human beings, and about this thoroughly
conflicted social condition they all share? Xenochronic combinations of
scenes and ideas recognize the broader implications of sexual and non-sexual
intimacy but leave them largely unresolved. The story seems to simply
resume 'forward' motion after an aside, and viewers 'follow.'

Ironies surround Tenoch's family home. Preconceptions of beauty, affluence, privilege, and security veneer the corruption and abuses of power that
provide for them. Workers in constant motion care for the home they are

unable to possess or enjoy, while family members themselves are mostly absent. Hanging out in a family room before going to a 'house party,' Tenoch, Julio, and Saba form a kind of surrogate family. They feign independence but are dependent on others. They are mostly insecure about their identities and their relationships but cover these ideas with half-lies, partial truths, and bravado. A full obtrusively oblique view depicts the trio smoking marijuana, drinking beer, and boasting about 'sexual conquests' they anticipate that night. There is at least limited trust among this group. Their statements to one another accumulate with the previous gradual disclosures of their sex-related interests; however, as they thrill themselves with ideas of fondling girls' (their friends' girlfriends') body parts, they playfully wrestle and pinch one another in a homoerotic rehearsal for their main events.

*Tu Mamá*'s voice-over and long-take techniques are extraordinary, particularly because they are sequentially aligned in conceptual continuity, but perhaps less distinctly the film frequently combines them with oblique angles. The oblique angle in this scene deflates the cinematic cliché of depicting the characters' drug-induced disorientation and subjectively skewed view on the world, like more classically in *Notorious* (Hitchcock 1946) or more radically in *Easy Rider* (Hopper 1969). Instead the oblique view reflects the adolescent characters' in-formation identities off-balance with the contested social conditions in which they struggle to navigate those formulations. Here, the oblique view dramatically revises intimacy amid a swirl of equally compelling social themes. It exposes and destabilizes their presumed heteronormativity and macho disrespect for the female partners they imagine as well as the repressed homoeroticism materially enacted in their wrestling game. The strange dialectics remain unsynthesized. The ironies highlight an indictment of the Mexican social condition that yields these social and political circumstances.

A 31-second long take depicts the aforementioned 'house party,' itself a trope of youth films and mythologized youth. A contrasting chain of lighting and colorization has linked the saturated red-browns of the Tenoch family room to the much brighter naturally lit garden where they smoke marijuana, and then to the hazy, blue-palleted party scene. The textures resonate against one another. At this house party Julio and Tenoch innocently dance together in one shadowy corner of the party, as similar small groups do elsewhere. The camera ambles room-by-room while the fifth voice-over entry states that Julio and Tenoch 'failed in their strategies for sexual conquest.' They participate in what Giddens explains as romantic love's 'quest' in binary-gendered terms where women seek out 'Mr. Right' and men aim to affirm traditional power dynamics through 'conquest' (1992: 10, 45–6). Sex facilitates the quest's/conquest's confirmation of one's destiny and identity (*ibid.*: 50). According to the narrator, 'they feared that this failure would set the tone for the rest of the summer.' *Tu Mamá*'s narration in this party scene recognizes Julio's and Tenoch's traditional love-sex views according to the limits of their knowledge and action—then exceeds them.

The stylized techniques liminally trace a threshold passage away from the characters and toward an assessment of the social conditions infiltrating the storyworld. Consequentially, the assessment of a 'failed' quest/conquest also prompts the possibilities of transformation and the potentialities of an emotional order based on mutuality. And there are no overly romanticized, magical real moments here.

After traversing a matrix of doorways and corridors, this long take ends by peeking in on Saba in a darkened room engaged in 'his first experience with group sex' [see Figure 6.5]. The mere mention of a teen orgy might seem exploitive or at least sensitive for some viewers. However, as in the film's opening sequence, the threshold annuls almost half of the frame, and the group-sex act appears as a tangle of body parts mostly in abstraction. Half seems revealed; more than half is hidden. In fact bodies contort and conceal parts of one another that defy clear visual representation. Even more clearly visible and slightly better lit are two unrelated partygoers, passed out in opposing directions on the floor to the left of the group-sex act and unaware or unfazed by the physical union. Certainly not sensationalistic in representation, this sexual narrative event all the more reflects a rite-of-passage act for Saba and propounds an exploration of intimacy toward processes of identity.

Without the narrator's explanation it might be difficult to discern details of this narrative event. Viewers might ask if that was sex. We cannot know,

*Figure 6.5* Mysteries Around Every Corner, It Seems

nor does it matter much, the extent to which this ascribes heterosexual-homosexual-polysexual identities for Saba or his partners, whether there was vaginal or anal intercourse, etc. Rather than a spectacle per se, and certainly not pornographic, the stylized instantiations of 'sexuality' here invite viewers to reimagine the structures by which we consider love and the mutual exchanges that sexuality can enact. It is transformationally 'questioning' for Saba and so for us.

Characters never discuss Saba's group sex event. It is unclear whether Julio and Tenoch even know about it. To whatever extent Saba's adolescent exploration of intimacy is 'successful' factors less in the larger reading than that it draws associations with comparably sexually charged narrative events like their three-way wresting match or like Julio and Tenoch engaging through quasi-public masturbation in their own imaginary group sex with Salma Hayek, their art teacher, and an imagined and exoticized-Spanish Luisa on the country club pool's diving boards. These events may remind viewers of proverbial *Penthouse* letters and pornography, but on another layer of the mythology their stylized treatments formulate a 'strange logic' that recodifies sex for intimacy. It recovers primordial considerations of intimacy. The hint of sensuality is part of the provocation. Rather than ignore or entirely divorce the social conventions and contexts, however, the scene's cinematic language that connects it in alternating stylistic treatments with neighboring scenes places the characters and their concerns in equal proportion with their environment and the social condition affecting them.

Many of the alterations for the R-rated version of the film reinstall troublesome aspects in mainstream generic treatments of adolescence and sexuality. Not to put too fine a point to it, censorship following traditional conceptions of romantic love reverts to structures and notions of love, sex, and identity that *Tu Mamá*'s poststructuralist advancements of confluent love precisely, systematically revise. Across a spectrum, each deserving dedicated interpretation, the straight, queer, latent-queer, and LGBTQ+ 'questioning' qualities of the story reach across heterosexual, homosexual, nonbinary, pansexual, sexual-tension-filled, intersexual, and asexual politics of intimacy as well as the possibilities of transforming them toward greater egalitarian values. 'Questioning' fuels explorations of identity.

The film offers early on incomplete activations in that process that Giddens describes as revolutionary transformations of intimacy. At her introduction during the wedding, Luisa appears largely as one more in a series of objects of fantasy for Julio and Tenoch. As the trio plans for and embarks on their road trip, she infuses hopefulness for confluent love, a love in Giddens' postmodern terms that is purer for its potentialities to explore mutuality and break traditional patterns leading to greater emotional orders. Growth is possible through 'developments.'

# 7 Development

*Tu Mamá* fuses and transforms genres.[1] More precisely, however, Act One initiates the youth movie aspects that then Acts Two and Three 'develop' through travel. Development, per the mythologies surrounding youthfulness but also as sociocultural concept more generally, takes our readings of *Tu Mamá* to a fork in the road. Divergent paths eventually travel in parallel directions with comparable points of destination. While travel seems comparable, the objectives (for Luisa, Julio, Tenoch, even Betsabé, and viewers) are leagues apart in contradistinctive realities. Ground-level traffic follows more directly material concerns regarding economic developmentalism, world-system politics, and allegorical relationships, but these diverge from another pathway exploring higher-order existential questions. As previously established, conceptual continuity with its abnormal logics can be multiply accessed through the film's youthful address to help navigate these two lanes of argument.

On both pathways, crucially, travel does not always directly correlate to forward progress: it encounters delays, detours, blockades, breakdowns; it encumbers getting lost and needing directions; it involves transfers, layovers, course corrections, circling around, and reversals; *ad nauseum*. Modernity in some respects is defined by just such experiences for many throughout the world in various expressions according to varying cultural logics, as it is too for adolescence.

Rather than one singularly unifying plot-point moment, a series of actions transition from Acts One to Two:

1. Tenoch and Julio shop for beer, snacks, and condoms;
2. they consult Saba on travel directions;
3. they pick up Luisa; and alternatively, Luisa readies for the trip and joins them;
4. they stop at the gas station;
5. our group embarks on the trip together.

The transitions occur xenochronically and reiteratively according to the filmmakers' notes (Cuarón and Cuarón 2001: 119–22, 197n24–6). This results in a tactful excess of information that merges youthfully intimate explorations with (im)material concerns of the road movie.

Two shots depict the group at the gas station. Consumerism thematically ties the *supermercado* to the *mega-gasolinería*, both highlighted by global-corporate branding and bigger-is-better mentality. These two locations particularly contrast materially with the family-owned businesses (including Chuy's and Mabel's) and more independent and private spaces frequented but imperiled throughout the film's story. Based on the linear-causal connections among actions, this mini-story does not seem terribly odd, and stylistically the two shots do not disrupt the sequencing even as much as the 4.5-second-average shots and continuity cutting at the *supermercado* previously did. Why is this information even presented? How, tactfully and practically, does this information serve the narrative? Do we just need fuel in our engine? For viewers sensitive to rationing and resource management, this is no small matter.

The first shot lasts about 18 seconds but consists of four grammatical parts: three 5-second stutter steps of Betsabé—pulling away from the pumps, pausing for Tenoch's return from the convenience store, but then pulling away twice again as a prank—then 3 seconds on him finally catching up. The bubbly pop song 'Insomnio' by Café Tacuba, lyrics suggesting mental states of insomnia and amnesia punned as travel on a 'forgotten path,' streams the alternatingly (dis)continuing action, but car sounds and Julio's intermittent guttural guffaws offer yet another rhythm to the montage. Luisa's patience runs out when she blurts curtly 'stop it.' The juvenile escapade stops (momentarily).

The prank compares with the one on Jano at the wedding, but salient details in this scene both distract from and secure the homology. Notably 'Pemex,' 'Comex,' and other corporate and state-subsidy markers juxtapose UNAM-Pumas and Zapatista stickers on the back windshield. Our view hovers over the backseat, in between and behind Julio and Luisa in the front seats (or, stopped and looking back, in front of them?) more focally aligned with a frustrated Tenoch outside the car. None of our characters suggest strong allegiances to any of the icons surrounding them nor their implied values (imperialism, corporate capitalism, hegemony, fundamentalism, nationalism), nor absolute resistance to them. Thereupon, they are beholding to the infrastructure containing all of them, as they were to wedding customs, for example, now paved as a road out of town.

A 4-second re-establishing shot shows Tenoch finally getting in the back seat after a frustrated retaliatory kick to Betsabé's door in proximity to Julio [see Figure 7.1]. Two dominant visuals compete for notice: a distant high-angle view on Betsabé now loaded with both fuel and

*Figure 7.1* Paved Paradise for a Parking Lot

identity-in-development passengers in lower-left juxtaposes the upper-right block of gas pumps. But probably going unnoticed is the field of bland-gray concrete connecting them all, our road-movie road (as commercial space and parking lot) and a background that refracts our material concerns. Even less noticed, a blanket of smog practically erases the looming mountains farthest in the background.

The aim is not efficient progress, for sure. Instead, reconsider the gas station scene alongside xenochronic events. Gassing the car is a material requirement for the road movie but rarely enters the plot. Here, within plot-point reiterations, it confounds connotations of 'developments' surrounding our (identity building, maturing) characters and responses to their multi-farious environments. With the next shot in on-the-road motion, Act Two fully underway, the narrative driving highway-speed literally and conceptu-ally *forward*, viewers may be inclined to not look back. Intermittent action and repeatedly emphatic transitional qualities bridge road and youth movie generic functions. Without absolute alignments but with strange dialectics, both parts contained by infrastructure and transported by Betsabé, competing notions of development interface within the reiterative plot-point moment.

The road movie generically relies on materially codifying tropes— driver-character, driving-agency, destination-revelation. Most object-materially stable are the road and the car themselves. *Tu Mamá* subscribes to and exponentially advances the function of the road's 'alternative space,' distant and distinct from the 'mainstream' enough to afford 'various transformative experiences' (Cohan and Hark 1997: 5). Our station wagon, too, particularly carries mid-20th-century connotations of suburbia, family outings, and the 'station' of middle-class privilege that provides and protects that lifestyle, which Betsabé maturates. Compelling interpretations of *Tu Mamá* extend many of the material concerns anchored by or emphasizing political economy to (trans)nationalism and collateral issues (Acevedo-Muñoz 2004; Saldaña-Portillo 2005). While these readings provide curbed clarity, they generally isolate particular issues and themes that reflect the film's own partial truths and siloed realities. Instead, through developments associated with youthful mythologies, the film's complex and multi-textural form exposes a network of social mechanisms and their values.

Genre studies further argue that character-plot development becomes a means of critique against 'conservative social norms' and the oppression of hegemony (Laderman 2002: 1; Cohan and Hark 1997: 1–3; Corrigan 1991: 144–6). David Laderman notes 'anti-genre sensibilities' that pit antithetical forces against one another—rebellion against conformity, conformity-in-nonconformity, liberation against restriction—around late-1960s countercultures and a 'precisely youth culture rebellion' (2002: 3, 19). New Hollywood's *Easy Rider* and *Bonnie & Clyde* (Penn 1967) as exemplars, the road movie's rebellion emulates a 'new' mainstream style because it 'evokes a countercinema in relation to classical narrative' (*ibid.*: 17). Somewhat ironically, this presumes an 'essential' U.S.-centered 'American-ness': 'a Hollywood genre that catches peculiarly American dreams, tensions, and anxieties, even when imported by the motion picture industries of other nations' (Cohan and Hark 1997: 10, 2). As the road movie travels to the Global South by the late 1990s, especially in *Tu Mamá* and *The Motorcycle Diaries* (Salles 2004), it challenges U.S.-dominant criteria.

Latin American road movies counter the individualistic quality of traditional road movies by alluding to collectivism and 'broader economic, historical, and national frameworks' (Garibotto and Pérez 2016: 8). Reassessing the functions of national/transnational/international and global contexts according to 'a dynamic dialogue across borders' begins to decenter the institutions, the arts, and their values maintained by prevalent world-system models, of which developmentalism and dependency theory are key ingredients (*ibid.*: 6–8). Even the mere appearance of manifestos in *Tu Mamá* likely reminds many viewers of the film cultures and discursive operations around New Latin American Cinema emerging around the late 1960s and that movement's militant politics in exposing the injustices of first-world presumptive standards imposed globally.[2] Yet *Tu Mamá*'s parodic stance updates the 'third cinema' politics, 'imperfect' aesthetics, even resistance to censorship with its own attention to fundamentals of developmentalism for 21st-century global-commercial audiences.[3]

As a concept, 'lack of development' likely serves greater purposes to the notions of maturity, emotional autonomy, and other mythological qualities of youthfulness in *Tu Mamá* even as it references 'underdevelopment' as a neoliberal political-economic condition that surrounds our characters. The film nonetheless fulfills the Latin American counter-generic strategies, exposing the binary structures associated with, among other issues, development, but then reinvents the processes of narration and resequences the narrative's material and de-materializing markers to invite (or at least demonstrate the possibility of) revolutionary transformation.

Returning to the fork in the road to which development delivers us, let us radically reconsider road movie aspects in relation to the mythologies surrounding adolescence and *Tu Mamá*'s youthful-sexual explorations of intimacy. Generically, the road stands as a 'universal symbol of the course of life' (Laderman 2002: 2). *Tu Mamá*'s road, as previously discussed, sometimes anchors character to Mexico's infrastructure, sometimes degrades to rocky paths and dirt roads, and sometimes lifts away from maps and geography principally. By the 1990s, road movies emote, according to Michael Atkinson, a postmodern anxiety by constituting an 'ideogram of human desire' (1994: 14–17). Timothy Corrigan comparably describes '*mise-en-abyme* reflection[s]' for audiences succumbing to 'historical hysteria' and no longer able to 'imagine naturalized history' (1991: 152–3). Treatments of Betsabé exemplify how *Tu Mamá* destabilizes automobile-related material concerns and shifts to psychic/spiritual explorations. Betsabé reconditions issues and values suggested traditionally as she is run-down, third-owner, driven-hard, and bartered for greater concerns. Her material form catalyzes non-material values. With her own highly referential name, humanistic 'panged' moment of profound growth, and especially knowledge of sexuality, car-as-character Betsabé aligns with the human characters and especially Luisa. Witnessing Betsabé's conscience and recognizing her material-immaterial conversions relieve pressure from other value-laden items in the road movie and throughout our film.

Nadia Lie proposes a new standard for Latin American genres, the 'counter-road movie' based on 'a more acute form of hampered movement' (2017: 15). Lie situates the counter-road subgenre according to a fused binary of mobility-versus-stasis, where narrative events like road blocks and police inspections, mechanical breakdowns, accidents, even cancelled plans, and absolute motionlessness formulate not just a brief dramatic punch of tension or conflict but the basis of the entire story and oftentimes curious resolutions (*ibid.*: 15–17). Crucially, Lie argues that travel routes and 'maps do not correspond to what they were supposed to represent,' and 'obstruction of movement is often compensated for by "imaginary travels"' (*ibid.*: 16–17). Surely a special lens refocuses *mise-en-abyme* psychic charges and cultural values across transnational paths. *Tu Mamá*'s youthful address grants 'ways of reacting to' these developments.

Having procured their beer, snacks, and condoms at the *supermercado*, a four-shot sequence compares our very different characters at journey's start. One two-shot scene reveals Julio and Tenoch consulting Saba on directions and travel plans, and the next two-shot scene officially brings Luisa into the shared journey. After a 10-second view of Saba's girlfriends in the back corner of the room, a 51-second long take depicts Saba giving travel directions to Julio and Tenoch. On the one hand, parts of his directions foretell the journey to be made—leave the city, go past Puebla, exit the toll highway for '*libre*'/'free' road to Oaxaca, once south find a road to the right and the beach, and miraculously 'there it is.' Equally portentous, his delivery is filled with strategic digressions of scattered details—the beautiful landscape, the military-police checkpoints, roadside signs, the shifts in security from city to southern state, the awe over things encountered during the journey. On the other hand, Julio and Tenoch doubt Saba's accuracy, and they have every right to. At one point they flip the map in front of them around and point toward the southwest for Oaxaca and not to the east and Veracruz. Saba confuses a river with a road on the map. Reason and realism are not his strong suits.

The sequencing lures viewers to wonder about Saba's lack of emotional maturity, cognitive development, rationality, or sobriety, but all the more it proves the inability of any known method (memory, historiography, cartography) to explain the spatio-temporal dimensions of the journey that lies ahead of our trio. The map appears foremost on a table, and the room is layered with a chaotic assortment of evocative items—drug paraphernalia, liquor bottles, dirty ashtray, left-overs from biology class demonstrations, and wall-hanger imagery of graffiti artwork, Che poster, Nirvana poster, Mexican national '*el tri*,' and an anarchy icon. As bohemian music plays under their conversation, the thematic dis-unification to this scene is amplified by the conceptual continuity of the sequence of action it both draws to a close (phone calls, travel arrangements) and opens up to reiterative and progressive intimate explorations on the road.

For Luisa, it was *different*. A 5.5-second high-angle view on Luisa sitting in a reading chair leads to an 82-second long take that follows her to answer the intercom, grab her duffle, tote-purse, and bottled water, and depart for the voyage she will make with Tenoch and Julio. Between these two shots Luisa remains noticeably framed by Jano's book *Fue sin Querer*, the book itself pretentiously and incongruously placed alongside a Yeats collection and canonical stacks in the earlier shot and a poster of the cover art ready to be hung in their living room in the latter shot. Recall the backhanded quality of this phrase as an apology: 'it was not what I wanted,' lacking full responsibility and sincerity. Surely only the most insecure author/person needs oversized reminders of self-worth literally filling each room of his house. Jano's mistakes and his refusal to acknowledge them, much less amend them, block Luisa's freedoms even in his physical absence. Borrowing Alfonso Cuarón's Godardian logic for the military-style blockades, perhaps Luisa cares about Tenoch's and Julio's developments because she is married to an under-developed husband, and they are all products of their society.

The first of these shots shows her eyes are closed. Luisa rests in peace but then comes back alive with the call from the teens to come downstairs. As a woman who sacrificed much of her childhood, coming awake reclaims a sense of youthfulness before it is 'too late.' As a woman in a compromised marriage, it represents the possibility of new self-discoveries. As a woman preparing to leave her unfaithful husband and embark on a scandalous, raucous adventure (adulterous sex with younger men!), she appears remarkably timid and proper. She models light khaki pants, a blouse and cardigan, and sensible travel shoes. She returns dirty dishes to the kitchen and brushes any dust and cigarette ash she may have left behind. She and Jano are still getting settled, and the apartment's clutter suggests an organized state of in-formation/information as much as it reveals a bricolage of personal items, souvenirs, family photos, with a heavy dose of Jano's academic-literary paraphernalia. The two consecutive apartments compare versions of clutter differentially for respective characters and their conditional development. That is, while there are no syntheses to these dialectics, the sequencing does expose the comportment of the characters and their dependence on shared, contrary conditions. The dialectics urge inciting questions.

The observing camera scans the bedroom after Luisa's exit and finds an open window. The final 32-second portion of this shot disassociates from character subjectivity—neither Jano's figurative dominance nor Luisa's physical existence—in the fourth-floor apartment space. A bird's-eye hovers above and overlooks the storyworld as Tenoch and Julio greet Luisa curbside, genially take her bag, and welcome her to the adventure. As they pull away from the curb, Betsabé ceases momentarily, perhaps second guessing the wisdom of this voyage, but then goes ahead—to the *megagasolinería* and the journey. The Cuarón brothers' Script Notes suggest that her malfunction must be subtle to avoid it being a gag, particularly with an automatic transmission (2001: 197 n23). Nonetheless, with whining engine and disbelief that she will mechanically survive the full trip, but without other recourse, the characters tentatively depart.

As a major plot-point moment, story information and action-following-action linearity disguise contests among the characters and significant contradictions bound into their social condition. Action often actually meanders; it reiterates; it starts and stops abruptly. Alternating stylistics disclose these as self-contradicting social mechanics and adherent values, which are to be critically explored over the journey.

Once on the road, the gradual disclosures of intimate information, initiating around the adolescent characters, refines with Luisa's inclusion. The typically benign 'so what do you do?' symbolically reiterates the earlier debate between Julio and Tenoch alone in traffic over the relative merits of their professional aspirations and adult expectations at the same time it simply enacts introductory polite conversations. Further, the polite question gestures toward a negotiation of understanding one another better, which is fundamental to mutuality. It also indicates healthy personal boundaries, balanced with social convention and decorum, which they acknowledge at the start of this journey (and different already from the trio's wedding/reception at first meeting). The boundaries are quickly tested by the incremental expressions of intimacy that follow, and greater honesty reveals itself, especially for and through Luisa.

The successive disclosures grow fairly quickly in the hothouse environment of their adventures:

1. the *Charolastro* pact;
2. how each treats their romantic-sexual partners;
3. whether they are faithful and why;
4. how sexually experienced each is;
5. which specific sexual techniques they have used and enjoy.

The progressively intimate disclosures balance against linear-causal actions. Although shaped by their macho arrogance and adolescent solipsism, Julio and Tenoch provide some genuine if partial answers to the questions and revelations. Luisa delivers the adolescents an adult-minded fresh air of revelation in turns. The gradual disclosures also cast light on the gaps in information, the previously unacknowledged disagreements, the half-truths, lies, and partial truths upon which Julio and Tenoch based their friendship and their very sense of 'being.'

Largely around travel down the road, with pauses and stops, several events coincide significantly with the developing reflections upon intimacies. A conjunction forms with Luisa explaining that she compromised her adolescence and professional aspirations to support her family, her admission of surprise that they guessed she could be a philosopher and 'that she looked like a thinker,' and their exit to the '*libre*' route. The style outweighs the characters' story-level demands. The voice-over narrator reveals her inner-most feelings and memories about her career, her marriage to Jano, and the insecurity she often felt around his pompous 'artistic' friends. Deep down she wanted to challenge them but 'never dared,' which the voice-over narrator, not Luisa herself, shares.

As the diegetic sound is lowered but not silenced entirely for this 11th voice-over narrator entry, Betsabé passes a Volkswagen Bug crowded with passengers dressed for their own ceremony, a bridal or *quinceañera* dress, perhaps, flowing out the window. The car itself has been ritualistically dressed too with flower streamers and ivory satin ribbons. The 'strange synchronization' of theme and form may not add up exactly at this moment in the narrative to a crystal-clear message, but what is clear are the ways each of these narrative events reiterate and then coalesce in forming relationships with loved ones. Stylistic exigencies prompt radical retrospection of the structures that can enable them—rite-of-passage birthday, marriage, domestic roles, even more general lifestyle choices and career decisions. These are part of the formation of adult identity, and they inform our possibilities for intimacy with others. Around mythologies of youth, they also hold in place values that deserve review.

The film's complex form systematically reveals our characters sharing intimate disclosures within their environment and as part of a larger social condition, but this happens selectively. As the trio sits for their first meal together, for example, the camera advantages briefly a beggar and later follows the Xochiapa townspeople working, dancing, and drinking in the back of the restaurant. The camera temporarily disregards the 'main' characters as much as the 'main' characters disregard these other characters. The next morning, Tenoch envisages his nanny's upbringing and home when they drive past her hometown of Tepelmeme, but he chooses not to stop and learn more nor even share this with the others. And before taking the adolescents (and Betsabé) to their breaking point on disclosures of sexual techniques, Luisa relates the tragic death of her first boyfriend, victim of a motorcycle crash at roughly the same age Julio and Tenoch are now. Their reactions prove this is a startling reminder of their own mortality and an existential awakening. This moment too—networked alongside the migrant bricklayer's corpse neglected four days before being claimed, the fatal crash of a chicken farmer's truck, many roadside commemorations, and more—fades from their thought. Travel on the road develops the progressive disclosures, and how they choose to act on these remains up for question.

Beyond being misdirected, detoured, and 'lost' most of the time, however, characters in this story frequently demonstrate in their relationships to ontological reality a profound uncertainty or an outright inability to 'know' certain kinds of information that many viewers expect as a matter of course. Intersecting with the road movie, the youthful address arrests differentiating structural codes to recover primordial inspiration for identity building processes. The material road parallels symbolic-immaterial and existential concerns, and the developments are systematically intermittent.

Consider three consecutive actions:

1.  passing a roadside check point;
2.  passing a mural;
3.  passing a field.

Passing a military-police roadside check point, Julio advises Tenoch to 'hide the stash,' referring casually to their illicit drugs. Tenoch replies 'it's cool.' But two other carloads of travelers are not as fortunate for whatever reasons: in juvenile terms, 'jeez, they got busted.' In the course of this 16-second long take, they consult one another: 'don't look at them' and 'don't turn around!' With its own agency outside the social forces of reproach and intimidation, the camera flaunts this advice: it looks where the characters do not dare and gazes in prolonged inspection. Reiterating the long look at Marcelino Escutia's corpse, this quasi-embodied view out the rear of the car completes the long take but converts its perspective through progressively greater objectivity. The shot quite literally makes the background a new foreground for renewed attention, so anamorphically the increasingly objective view transcends the diegesis and exposes several of the competing values associated with the social mechanism drawn out by allegory.

Classical paradigm tendencies prod viewers to read the scene, primarily, motivated according to the stakes for Tenoch, Julio, and Luisa and then, secondarily, as what David Bordwell calls a 'little dissertation' on, for example, individual rights in Mexico or the world, on the ironies of lawlessness and corruption in Mexican and global institutions, or even on the decriminalization of one's 'stash' (1985: 52). Instead, the duration of the single take travelling 'forward' through the film's sequencing but also looking back 'clashes' with graphic directionality and chronotopical logic in sequence. It suspends the social mechanisms through which traditional values of human rights, national citizenship, and legal rights may be contemplated anew.

Passing a roadside mural, next, initiates several remarkably incongruous pronouncements: '*El respeto al dererecho ajeno es la paz*,' 'Peace means respect for the rights of others.' The well-known national dictum by Benito Juárez appears in bold type over a three-part vignette of clear sky across top, mountains across bottom, and a bust of Juárez seeming to crop up from the fertile land at right. In front of the dimensionally flat but oversized imagery of the mural, workers line from left to center. The trajectory left-to-right follows a worker-driven tractor in slow progress up the road. One aspect of the legacy of Juárez was that he became president in 1858 by succession mandated by the newly minted Constitution of 1857, an age of Mexican government lasting to the next modern constitutional reform in 1917. Mid-19th-century Mexican capitalism buoyed by liberal-democratic ideals stands up for comparison to contemporary globalization in this shot. The long shot shows this mural in lower left as Betsabé and her companions travel left to right on a stretch of road, and mountains and clear sky fill the top two thirds of the frame. The ambivalence is rich. This *mise-en-abyme* view implies a hopeful parallel between the Mexican statesman's proclamation of respect for equal rights and our travelers but also seems inefficacious given the previous shot's check-point social forces. The dialectics grow strange. Questions are left open for viewers.

The long-take sequencing continues as do the unresolved juxtapositions. Presumably some miles down the road from the checkpoint and the mural, Betsabé appears in left-to-right motion from a ground-level long view in a graphic collision with a horse-pulled cart moving right-to-left. First, viewers wonder, are we learning what 'only the locals know,' as promised at the wedding? Second, this defies romantic 'postcard' beauty, the stereotype, and tourist gazes in favor of Mexico's contested social condition. Third, the preponderance of graphic-visual collisions in and across shots in this and similar sequences ballast our readings with mainstream preferences for spectacle. By these plot-point moments in the story, some viewers may half-expect Betsabé and our travelers to actually crash into one of the many vehicles and pedestrians in intersecting motion around them. Viewers may be looking for some action.

These shots serve a sequence that delivers Luisa noticing and somewhat indiscreetly calling attention to the stray erection Tenoch gained while napping. (He appears unable or unwilling to 'hide his stash.') At first slightly embarrassed, Tenoch eventually responds to Julio, singing out, 'you got a woody?' The two adolescents spur one another and inadvertently divulge to Luisa that they have inspected each other's genitalia, measured them, and debated their attractiveness. Notably, like in their country club shower antics and swimming contests, they cannot agree even on the factual bases and metrics upon which to form their opinions. This is light-hearted but also puerilely competitive. Given the closeness of their friendship, the disclosures might reveal a limited but shared trust.

With sexual connotations surrounding the actions, the disclosures emphasize more directly (homo)sexual tension. As Luisa's initial reaction suggests, the exchange of intimate, normally private information may be surprisingly unconventional in macho terms and at least vaguely homoerotic. However, Luisa reshapes the conversation's exchange of intimate information as affirmations of identity. She is reaffirmed in her emotional autonomy. She revises confidence in sexual identity for the adolescents by describing an uncircumcised penis as '*qué rico*,' subtitled as 'yummy!' in suggestively fellatious terms. In overview, she guides them to disclose their genuine selves, even through unexpected intimate details, and face those consequences.

A shot-countershot series within this sequence depicts this conversation, but it never matches character-to-character. That is, Luisa's passenger-seat view on Julio in driving seat shows him looking out the windshield, not back to her; Julio's view on Luisa shows her waking up and in reaction looking outside the car; Luisa's view on Tenoch in backseat shows him waking up and looking toward Julio; Luisa's gaze on Tenoch's erection is from Julio's vantage; Tenoch's countershot shows him looking toward the rear compartment; and Julio's quick glance to see Tenoch's 'woody' is from Luisa's vantage. By classical paradigm standards, the continuity appears slightly off. Rather than set and develop, the stageline seems to pivot and constantly reset. Rather than anchor in characters' perspectives, these shots circulate the interior space of Betsabé. Rather than consolidate subjective views for a consistent logic in this scene, the perspectives fracture with individual interests and considerations of the intimacy being disclosed. The soundtrack even toys with this idea with diegetic 'road music,' Brian Eno's entrancing 'By This River.' As the batteries in a portable CD player die, the music digitally skips, glitches a few seconds, then silences. The characters remain as incognizant of their environment and its social conditions as they are apart from one another during this exchange.

Luisa follows a slight lull in the conversation, hesitates in deliberation, and then dares to ask Julio and Tenoch, 'how do you make love to your girl-friends?' Some viewers caught in the lull will find the question provocative, but it figures with 'developments' and disclosures of intimacy. The question advances transformational possibilities of confluent love by prioritizing *ars erotica*, the refinement of techniques aiming at mutual pleasure in sexuality. The question stands in clear defiance of what viewers have previously seen, one reality in which the adolescents engage in sexual activity with little concern for technique nor their partners' pleasure. The question also reiter-ates the issue of prostitution, a traditionally objectifying enterprise designed around providing sexual services without intimacy, from '*la reina*' stop. The social-conventional 'impurity,' shame, and hypocritical concealment sur-rounding prostitution converts here to 'purer' opportunities through sexual technique to mutually engage a partner in reciprocal identity building (Gid-dens 1992: 82–4, 120–3).

Unaware of their own naiveté, Julio and Tenoch boast in tag-team response that they 'know every trick,' how to do 'everything,' 'the whole *Kama Sutra*,' the quintessential placeholder for sexual-technique compre-hensiveness. Luisa dispels their adolescent, macho arrogance with a light touch. And even Betsabé pops her cork.

## Notes

1. See Finnegan (2007: 31), Tierney (2018: 82–90), and Davis (2014).
2. For a fuller discussion on Mexican and Latin American cinema traditions and world-system politics, see Baugh (2004a, 2004b).
3. See Ana M. López (1990) on parody, developmental theory, and New Latin American Cinema.

# 8  Sex (It Bears Repeating)

*Tu Mamá* depicts a wide variety of sexual events. Its conceptual continuity repeats aspects among these events in relation to our understanding of the oftentimes contradictory and disarmingly complex character-plot developments. Equally challenging, *Tu Mamá*'s sexuality and resulting questions of intimacy can be extrapolated to allegorical and symbolic dimensions accumulating as multifaceted messages. Political and cultural allegories may be slightly easier to locate, even though the landscape and maps are shifting on top of one another, but the existential and more ecstatic transferences are worth discovery all the more.

Having made detours to the '*libre*'/'free' road, been slowed by various traffic and road blocks, and made necessary stops for food and rest, the journey encounters a momentarily insurmountable obstacle. Betsabé's breakdown—mechanical but also, surprisingly, expressive—initiates a chain of integrated actions. In plot order:

1. Luisa meets Doña Martina;
2. Luisa and Tenoch have sex, and Julio accidentally observes;
3. Julio and Tenoch swim together naked;
4. Julio confesses/brags to Tenoch about covertly having sex with Ana;
5. Tenoch demands appropriate explanation and apology;
6. Luisa and Julio have sex, and Tenoch distantly observes;
7. Tenoch retaliates by proving he secretly had sex with Ceci;
8. Julio demands appropriate apology;
9. Luisa demands amendments;
10. the group resumes its excursion to heaven-on-Earth.

On their own, these narrative events are dramatic and at times even potentially salacious. But together and contextualized, they ramp up the progressive disclosures of intimacy among our travelers and formulate tests of maturity for their in-formation and in-crisis identities.

A 231-second hand-held long take depicts the sexual rendezvous between Luisa and Tenoch. The camera first observes a distraught, sobbing Luisa alone in her motel room as Tenoch innocently arrives. Julio is showering, Tenoch wearing only a towel is ready for his shower, and he comes only to borrow shampoo. With greater maturity than he has previously expressed to any adult, Tenoch fully acknowledges Luisa, asks if she is okay, and shows her compassion. Their mutual consideration rehabilitates their first meeting at the wedding reception. Luisa brushes away her tears and asks Tenoch if she can see his body and his aforementioned erection, which was an explicit topic of conversation during their car ride. The view of the scene borrows from Luisa's perspective at the start from high over-shoulder, but then roughly standing-eye-level tracks back to the functional equivalent of an establishing shot. As the long take runs on, camera placement merges multiple identifications across subjective and objective perspectives as well as shrouding much of the frontal nudity. She admits that she has 'imagined' what Tenoch would look like nude, and Luisa's actions are less about seduction or even *scientia* instruction and much more extensions of the gradual disclosures of intimacy the group has experienced over their trip together.

Teenage sex that opens *Tu Mamá* is thoroughgoingly romantic: it is bound by its own traditional values. Romantic sex 'brackets off the *ars erotica*,' where identity affirmation and sexual satisfaction are 'supposedly guaranteed' by fantasy, destiny, and erotic forces but unequally distributed according to gender between male and female partners and traditional roles (Giddens 1992: 62). By contrast, confluent sex

> introduces the *ars erotica* into the core of the conjugal relationship and makes the achievement of reciprocal sexual pleasure a key element in whether the sexual skills, the capability of giving and experiencing sexual satisfaction, on the part of both sexes, become organized reflexively via a multitude of sources of sexual information, advice, and training.
> (*ibid.*: 62–3)

*Tu Mamá*'s specially branded parametric narration discloses the parameters of sexual events and their progressive intimacies.

A scene matching Luisa and Tenoch together reiterates the vignette: this time Julio gaining a stray erection during a travel nap, and Luisa recognizing it and propositioning him. And like Julio's sex scene with Ceci—and unlike Tenoch's with Ana and then with Luisa both in long take—this sex scene with Luisa is maintained by stylized continuity editing. A pair of establishing shots show Tenoch pulling onto a dirt road that, according to a road sign, will lead to 'Puerto Suelo,' translated 'port of ground,' oxymoronically water-land. The film's cartography suggests that this turn-off would be near Mexico's actual Laguna de Manialtepec, a relatively remote coastal lagoon near Puerto Escondido named after a Náhuatl phrase for 'the hill where water is born.' Geographically, Laguna de Manialtepec's spring-fed shallows are dotted by small islands of mangroves that during rainy seasons open to the ocean, and the place is known as an ecotourist destination for an algae that on rare occasion glows bioluminescent. *Tu Mamá*'s story does not travel there, however, and it certainly does not paint a lush magical-real backdrop for the sexual rendezvous. Miracles nonetheless will occur.

This dusty road paradoxically appears as a passageway but then is blocked and heavily washed-out. Angry and hurt by what he perceives as betrayals by either Luisa or Julio or both, Tenoch cuts the engine and marches to the other side of the road in a class-tinged tantrum, yet he cannot help from spying on the sex scene either. A series of cross-cut shots divide our interests between Tenoch's sulking and the union of Luisa and Julio. Like Tenoch, Julio reveals a new expression of more mature compassion but for Tenoch, not for his present partner Luisa. As he did with Ceci, Julio acquiesces to Luisa's allure anyway.

A 63-second shot finally anchors this 108-second shot-countershot scene in the action of sexual intercourse [see Figure 8.1]. Perhaps even more patiently and emphatically after Tenoch's less than rewarding experience, Luisa invites Julio to 'go slow' and to 'look' and 'feel' the sexual experience for greater engagement. Overexcited Julio begins with a stammering, incomprehensible first-person 'Yo-Yo-Yo-Yo-Yo-,' suggesting he wants to undress her ('let me') but instead just scattering fragmented inarticulations 'I-I-I-I-I-'

*Figure 8.1* Erasure, Clash With Intimacy

as solipsistic incomplete thoughts. Meaningless Morse code repeats. And in counter-rhythm with this punctuated dialogue and performance, the car's radio plays a *cursi*/corny Mexican pop song. But like with Ceci, Julio's presence diminishes. Literally sitting beneath Luisa on top, Julio slumps down into the car seat beneath the window frame out of the camera's view.

Whatever is 'sexy,' 'seductive,' or 'steamy' is overridden by the attempted fair exchange of intimate knowledge. One try after another, Luisa invites her companions to engage in confluent love, to bring physical closeness in contact with being 'closer' through mutual appreciation and respect. These two sex actions are opportunities for exploring one another's in-process identities and the potentialities for greater equality among the three of them.

Luisa engaging in sex with first Tenoch and then Julio hints at her recovery of a lost youth and some psychic healing, especially given her physical ailment and short future. Her sex with Julio specifically aims to restore 'a natural balance' that she fears she may have disrupted. Her intentions are good throughout, she apologizes afterward for hurting either of them incidentally, and regrets any possible mistakes. In this behavior she models the genuine maturity of an in-process and imperfectly human adult identity through a conception of confluent love, of which Tenoch and Julio are in sore need. Her sexual behavior with Julio and Tenoch further disrupts the type of traditional models that hold these characters in their social condition.

As the voice-over narrator's 17th entry explains Luisa's hope at restoring balance to their group, the shot centers on the trio sitting together over dinner but begins with the working hands over a stove that made that dinner and ends with two plumbers at work on a bathroom sink. As in previous voice-over entries, faint diegetic sounds underlie the narrator's hypodiegetic voice to remind viewers that this story does not begin and end with our 'main' characters. The characters' stories coincide with their environment. Luisa's intervention incites transformative possibilities pointedly for the trio but by extension too for their social condition. Her impending death weighs heavy on her mind even if Tenoch and Julio (and viewers) are only partly aware of this truth. And it places in bold relief the stakes of the humanistic questions our characters have as a result of their intimate interactions.

Explaining to Tenoch her decision to have sex with him, Luisa claims that 'the same thing would have happened if Julio had come to my room.' Luisa exemplifies the idea of a confluent-contingent relationship over and above the traditional-romantic love with the ideal mate. To the extent that these two sex scenes are seductive, they induce a sexual arrangement aiming at emotional exchanges and mutual understanding. Where seduction, like Ceci's of Julio, simply reverses the competitive romantic-love power dynamic in favor of the female-seductress, Luisa's agency attempts to restructure the love-sex action and permutate it with values toward the possibility of new emotional orders. Tenoch's suggestions that she 'shouldn't' have sex with anyone but him and that he is a 'sap' reflect his unconscious adherence to romantic love and the traditional power structures implied by it. Never mind that these claims also overlook his own hypocritical act of having sex with not just a married woman but his own cousin's wife.

Luisa tries to bring Tenoch into an alignment with her, but he kicks the bed out of the way and loses himself in a tangle of bodily appendages [see Figure 8.2]. The *mise-en-scène* formally reveals the cross-purposes of the characters. Julio, too, initially graphically in-line with Luisa, frantically throws her aside the car's backseat for the mechanics of undressing and insertion, and then he sinks mostly out of view in self-effacement. Neither adolescent character fully reconciles this opportunity to align with Luisa.

Both prematurely ejaculate in stupendous fashion. Julio's eyes roll back in his head almost unaware of Luisa's physical being. Tenoch exclaims in clearly Freudian terms '*¡mamacita!*' Both are quick to apologize, and each apology is with '*perdón,*' not with the earlier self-aware mockery of '*fue sin querer.*' Genuine apologies, they seem to express a greater sense of self-deprecation and insecurity around their adult identities and intimate interactions in this specific instance.

These two intergenerational heterosexual events are best initially read as mostly failing tests of maturity for Julio and Tenoch and a laudable attempt at regaining hopeful growth by Luisa. Much of the two long-take shots in question are censored in the R-rated version of the film and erase not just some sexually explicit material but the very bases of our characters'

*Figure 8.2* Misalignments, Clash With Intimacy

explorations of intimacy and consequential identity building processes. Unlike in the previous sex scenes with their girlfriends, in these scenes Luisa hopes to prove the value of arousal, foreplay, and pleasure but toward mutual exchange with the sexual partner. The film's intricate system of stylistic devices elevates the representation beyond the superficiality of sensationalism and spectacle. Luisa's *ars erotica* puns fabulously with the parametric-cinema 'techniques' of the Cuarón brand coded into sequential chains.

*Tu Mamá* presents a kind of xenochronic syllogism over this sequence. In the character realm, the sexual-romantic qualifications in the two bilateral sex scenes with Luisa correlate with Julio and then Tenoch boasting/confessing and then apologizing to one another for past indiscretions. That Julio and Tenoch each had sex with the other's girlfriends, first, operates outside the *Charolastra* code but is entirely predictable as they are young men ruled by their hormones and macho one-upmanship. That the actions are actual sexual infidelities according to social convention and infractions of their manifesto also speaks to the adolescent characters' overreliance on simplified scripts that cannot account for their terribly complex and transitory world. Their surprise at each other's indiscretions further reflects their naiveté and inexperience, but also their revelations and possibility for change.

If sex with Luisa puts pressure on Tenoch and Julio to learn and grow, attempts at confluent sex with them in turn for Luisa correlates in a strange logic with all she learns from Doña Martina and her granddaughter Luisita and will learn from Mabel, Chuy, and their family. Giving alms, we recall, was a basis of Luisa's backstory, a personal sacrifice for another's good and an attempt at restoring 'natural balance,' which correlates with her panged moment of profound growth. Almost a throw-away image, our trio's first evening in Xochiapa instantiates the act of 'donation' that reiterates throughout the story. Luisa guides Tenoch and Julio through gift-giving to the beggar and then respectfully and dearly concludes the exchange '*adiós*,' 'goodbye' but with subtle 'blessing to God.' From Doña Martina, Luisa may find a similar appreciation for generosity and *caritas*, which Julio and Tenoch mostly overlook, even in the face of sacrifice and painful loss. *Tu Mamá* propounds resounding lessons on charity, friendship, love of family, and more well beyond 'sexy' treatments.

For Luisa, the tests for intimacy also recall the kinds of juvenile interactions she has endured with Jano in the marriage she is escaping. The hope she has in the youthfulness of Julio and Tenoch to overcome the burdens of traditions comes-and-goes quickly across episodes. Conceptual continuity delivers this diegetic information but also lifts above it as well to clarify the limits of our characters in their social condition. The varying rhythms across convoluted layers of the story emphasize what the characters remain unable to do: expose their genuine motivations and share intimate aspects of their lives in mutually respectful and caring ways. These, too, imbricate but transcend social mechanics, conventions, and rituals.

Recall another strange syllogism, like the matching sex scenes with Luisa. *Tu Mamá* includes twin swimming contests. The earlier race was at Tenoch's father's country club. Julio's invitation to the club is contingent on his friendship with Tenoch, and Tenoch's depends on his family's privileges. Contradictory notions of exclusion-inclusion, diversion-routine, and freedom-restriction oscillate throughout the club space. That first country club sequence subtly revises continuity editing by presenting, first, a high-angle, slightly oblique establishing shot with sharply angled visual weights that boldly direct Tenoch leading Julio down the off-balance pool pathway. Outside-in editing delivers the teens to poolside lining up to begin their race and counting in unison, '*uno-dos-¡tres!*,' typical for child-like games for mutually adjudicating the rules. The soundtrack across these shots offers a number of abrasive patterns and competing rhythms—a hushed metronomic sprinkler against the hypodiegetic voice-over, then point-of-audition sounds for underwater action, followed by water-surface splashes.

The polyrhythmic editing at the pool shifts strikingly to a 33-second long take of Julio and Tenoch showering in individual stalls, then examining and discussing Julio's genitalia with abandon, and finally resorting to a game of naked tag. They debate swimming strategies and dispute race results. In spite of all their similarities, Tenoch and Julio disagree over the metrics of the empirical results: the winning distance is 'just two meters' or 'ten at least,' then 'four max,' so compromising, 'let's call it eight.' Strikingly, their competitions climax in homosexually charged barbs and the invective 'faggot,' betraying their own hate-filled immaturity but dismissed waggishly.

In its own strange logic, the two country club scenes (swimming contest and later masturbating on the diving boards) dialogue with one another—most directly as before-and-after encountering Luisa. Xenochronic polylogics (dialogues, triads, etc.) draw associations across scenes at the club with the swimming contest much later in our story at the Teposcolula motel. Although not immediately 'sexual,' homoeroticism, competitiveness, and similar collateral issues across these scenes form a network of associations that ultimately drive at issues of intimacy and the processes for growth and revolutionary progress. Exceeding dramaturgy, the film's style detains differentiating structures surrounding love, sex, and intimacy to expose and reformulate their networked valuations. Compelling issues themselves, the mythologies they form are bewildering yet more significant.

In between their respective sexual engagements with Luisa, Tenoch and Julio conduct a second swimming race in the motel pool. Like at the country club, underwater photography and point-of-audition sound ironically situates viewers equally, paradoxically, with both characters but relieves their full subjectivity. The visuals temporarily but even more starkly disassociate our view from the above-water social circumstances. This race, unlike at the club, is more fully in open public but still in constricted, even intimate space; they are both naked; and leaves and natural detritus surround them in the murky-gray water. Their competition is primal if not fully 'primordial.' It is at this point that our 15th and 16th voice-over entries consecutively explain the 'panged' moments of profound growth our characters experienced, things they 'couldn't understand' but viewers must try to.

Camera placement along the stagelines and long takes subtly alter the conventional continuity-based editing that depicts Julio and Tenoch each in turn struggling with their self-discoveries. In both cases, the voice-over narrator explains, as children Julio and Tenoch each repressed the painful feeling and refused to discuss it with anyone else. These two pangs of betrayal indicate moments of growth involving intimacy gained, recognized, but then lost, revalorized, and redefined. For both Julio and Tenoch, they specifically recall memories of feeling betrayed by parents and the overly idealized trust that, as children, they wanted to place in their parent but learned they could not. These are quintessentially adolescent lessons, and they introduce profound questions for Julio and Tenoch. Luisa and even Betsabé experienced similar incidents, learning life-altering lessons from personal loss. Denying easy answers, the questions stress hopeful transformations in asking inciting questions. As part of the film's youthful address, the pangs, individualized gut-level lessons and moments of conscience, reiteratively reflect on the social condition all characters, 'main' and 'minor' and young and adult alike, encounter in this millennial Mexican-global culture.

Linear-causal connections among events and actions as well as some generic qualities gloss over these more complex aspects of *Tu Mamá*. Far from immediately apparent, confluent sexuality, even in obscured glimpses and brief mentions, helps to decipher the values of intimacy. The character most likely to be objectified through sexual sensationalism in this film, withstanding Hollywood's patriarchal and heteronormative traditions, Luisa remains the strongest character-agent for the transformational possibilities of intimacy in *Tu Mamá*'s storyworld. Her story, as viewers know by end, is short-lived. The film's mid-narrative plot point and structural hinge occurs as Luisa meets Doña Martina, a 98-year-old woman who, according to Luisa, 'remembers everything since she was five.' Her envisagement resembles an oracle. With Betsabé needing repair, the trio is delayed in their travels at Teposcolula and has the opportunity to interact with its citizens. Experiences here seem light-years from modern Mexico City.

After seeing Luisa laughing aloud at Betsabé's timely radiator burst, and perhaps equally at the comically serious efforts of Julio and Tenoch to throw bottled water into the convulsing radiator, an establishing shot resets the scene in this small southern-Mexico village. The cacophony of screaming, laughing, hissing, and car-radio music converts with the cut to the repetitive-meditative 'hum' of a tractor towing in Betsabé. Julio rides alongside the tractor driver, Tenoch follows behind on foot, all moving right-to-left, which ends with a quick graphic collision with an out-of-town bus pulling into a stop left-to-right. Luisa lies motionless on the car hood as if she is as 'dead' as Betsabé's inoperative engine. The procession predicts the funeral the group will pass on their way out of town later, adding to our ritual-associational networks.

Julio offers a cigarette and then receives the gift of a hat from one older man. Julio wears a graphic t-shirt with an iconic eagle and the words 'northern pride' in English, while the man wears a serape. A visual dialectic between Julio and this local citizen in front-center parallels Tenoch arguing with the mechanic over car repairs in background-left. Other than that, throughout this scene Julio and Tenoch interact only with one another in their typical childish rapport—playing with toys and snickering over the poster of a male nude sculpture. At first it appears Luisa's interactions will instill a political dynamic not that much different from the adolescents', just with greater sophistication.

She accepts a coconut water from a local woman wearing an apron who replies to Luisa's thank you '*gracias*' with '*con permiso*.' Subtitling ignores this comment entirely, and non-Spanish-speaking audiences likely will too. Rather than the social convention of 'you're welcome' or 'nothing to it' in '*de nada*' for example, this reply instead apologizes and defers the rights of the server to Luisa. The '*con permiso*' compares with the '*perdón*' characters state in this film at key moments (like after premature ejaculation and during feelings of low self-worth) but is strikingly different from the self-aware pranking of '*fue sin querer*.' Literally 'with your permission,' idiomatically 'please excuse me,' this reply speaks to recurrent privilege and class station in millennial-Mexican social conditions. At least three contradictory realities—that of Julio and Tenoch, that of the local citizens, and one in flux for Luisa—meet at this location, a contact-point.

The preceding shot showed the adolescents in their respective interchanges with locals, a pairing of dialectical relationships, and now viewers can situate that view more firmly—and arguably as firmly as any first-person throughout the film—in Luisa's revisionary perspective. This shift to a brief but relatively clear character-based perspective stands apart from the film's usual confluence of access points and barrage of multiple identifications for viewers, and it matches with the most thoroughgoing inter-personal transformation of intimacy. The point-of-view quality also xenochronically forecasts the film's only second-person shot amidst climaxes later as Luisa dances into the camera.

An over-the-shoulder view through Luisa's vantage traces a bricolage of items, ostensibly an *ofrenda* (religious offering) but also, in the market space, some previously owned personal items, souvenirs, trinkets, several with varying degrees of transactionally spiritual significance translated as products for barter or resale. The camera lines down her arm as it reaches for and her hand grasps a small white stuffed-toy mouse wearing a pink and calico dress hand-embroidered 'Luisa.' At first glance it appears entirely insignificant, a child's long-lost, long-forgotten plaything. Luisa notices and shares with the older local woman selling it, 'That's *my* name.' In shot-countershot exchange, the older woman replies with her own personalized significance only partly disclosed: 'Luisita. Pretty name.' Unlike so many food servers, mechanics, plumbers, and workers before, this woman is named for us, Doña Martina, and her local knowledge is prized rather than deferred or ignored (by Luisa). The call-and-response exchange of connections to the name merely hints at the intimacy and wisdom the older woman conveys to Luisa, who then tries to adopt and reapply it in the short life she knows she has remaining. The narration does not disclose this easily. Instead, viewers must interpret this elusive part of the story through Luisa and her condition.

Luisa's in-process emotional maturity shines through this sequence, particularly in comparison to her companions but also as it seems she has no time to waste. Luisa's actions and concerns may not immediately register with sexuality, and yet xenochronic associations draw on comparable stakes, intimate transformations among our characters. Her near-saintliness amplifies the existentialism at stake for the travelers as well as up for question for viewers. Moreover, the piety and selflessness might reverberate with allegorical meaning once the story reaches 'Heaven's Mouth.'

Learning from Doña Martina reflects Luisa's role as an agent of confluent love. She learns of Doña Martina's dearly departed granddaughter, Luisa's namesake Luisita Obregón, who perished while trying to cross the border from Mexico to the United States. Although tempting, pinning this part of the story to international policy on immigration too strictly overlooks the primordial insights it traces with similar identity building processes around intimacy. 'Luisa' on the toy does not reference only *our* Luisa, as Luisa first suggests, nor does it merely reference Doña Martina's late granddaughter or her circumstance. The references alert viewers to referentiality. The name enacts an exploration of intimacy between two mutually respectful adults; it recodes the existential questions these characters have and the mortal existence they (and we all frequently) take for granted.

Ironically telling of their romance and marriage, Luisa's most intimate exchange with Jano occurs long-distance by a pay phone and as a voicemail on their answering machine following her encounter with Doña Martina.

His absence affords Luisa a chance to explore a new emotional order in which she restructures the functions of love and intimacy. At first her voice is heard over visuals of a roadside storefront where Julio and Tenoch display their immaturity and ignorance of Luisa's condition. The hand-held camera moves right eventually 'meeting' her and showing her alone in an old-fashioned phone booth. Her voice-over comes to match her on-screen presence. In some respects, this retrofits her objectified 'reception' at the wedding. She admits that she 'wanted to vanish' from his life, leaving no note without the concern of worrying him. But she realizes that is 'not right.' Beyond confessing her mistakes and making amends, tabulating a moral-ethical point, she consolidates a larger existential lesson from Doña Martina as the visuals reincarnate as a 'walking' long take through their empty home. 'Imagine everything she's experienced,' Luisa shares. After a pregnant pause, she emphasizes the greater self-disclosure and lesson for all: 'and everything a person never gets to experience.'

The invisible-visible presence in the images of Luisa exemplify systemic patterns whereby *Tu Mamá* advances a disarming counter-narrative. More precisely, narrative and counter-narrative lines cooperate with transidentifications across them. Aspects of characters can be defined frequently by their material-object surroundings and conspicuously dated forms of communication but then may be negated abruptly. Thematic and formal repetitions and stutters across the narrative might be considered analogously with glitches. Where representational narrative and social systems operate toward 'completion, perfection, and control' that formulate a 'sealed triad under conditions of modernity,' according to Sean Cubitt, the glitch evidences that 'control is never complete' (2017: 20). A prevalent 21st-century 'digital logic' (read: binary code as logic and aesthetics) pretends 'autonomy' and a 'wholly rational existence' (*ibid.*: 25–6).

Glitches likely cannot provide passage to heaven. Yet beyond their high-tech connotations, glitches help explain the reiterative actions and events in *Tu Mamá* as disturbances to millennial unified/unifying systems of representation, narrative, and community. Disturbances can provide a 'decolonial' counter to hegemonic singularity and put human subjectivity 'in question' (*ibid.*: 20, 26). Meandering, repeating actions, stuttering, and stalling-out, like glitches, enact a form of '*indifference* underpinning the logic of exchange': 'liminality operates between the smoothed and insensible operation' of codes of representation, narrative, and the social world (*ibid.*: 26). For Luisa particularly after her experiences with Doña Martina but also for *Tu Mamá* as a whole, transforming intimacy must be considered as on-going processes. Identity developments are not just repeating but ever-becoming.

# 9 'Mí Manifiesto'

| | | |
|---|---|---|
| 1. | ¡No follaré con vosotros! Vosotros podéis follar entre vosotros si os apetce. | I'm not fucking either of you. You can fuck each other if you want. |
| 2. | Voy a tomar el sol en pelotas y no quiero teneros como perros encima de mí. | I'm going to sunbathe nude, and I don't want you sniffing around like dogs. |
| 3. | Yo escojo la música. | I pick the music. |
| 4. | En el momento en que yo diga os calláis la boca. | The moment I ask, kindly shut your traps. |
| 5. | Vosotros cocináis. | You two cook. |
| 6. | No quiero escuchar ni saber nada de vuestras pobrecitas novias. | Not another word about your poor girlfriends. |
| 7. | Si yo os lo pido, tenéis que estar al menos a diez metros de distancia, o si lo prefiero a más de 100. | If I ask, you're to stay ten yards away. Or 100, if I prefer. |
| 8. | Vosotros os encargáis de toda labor física. | Obviously, you do all the manual labor. |
| 9. | Sólo podéis hablar de temas en los que estéis de acuerdo, pero es mejor si habláis lo menos posible. | No discussing things you don't agree on. Better yet, just keep your mouths shut. |
| 10. | Prohibido contradecirme y menos empujarme. | You're not allowed to contradict me, much less push me! |

Luisa's 'Mí Manifiesto,' personalized 'My Manifesto,' echoes 'The Charolastra Manifesto' Julio and Tenoch share with Luisa at the start of their journey. Its repetition likely prompts viewers subscribing to classical paradigm procedures to immediately compare-contrast the itemized points and the overall arguments (if there are any clear overall Charolastra arguments beyond self-inflicted contradiction). Also when slowed to the pace of historical reflections, mentioned before, the mere appearance of the manifestos summon legacies of the New Latin American Cinema and comparable political-art cultural expressions. But for Tu Mamá, it was different.

*Tu Mamá* repeats itself. Sometimes it loops, stutters, or glitches; sometimes it resounds in full voice. The repetitions adhere to a logic that amounts to *reiterations*. That is, *Tu Mamá* recasts certain narrative parts (themes, actions in linear-causal relation, matching events, even stylistic patterns and narration schemes) as sequenced reformulations that prompt radical retrospection and originary hermeneutics, particularly here around in-formation identities according to sex and film-genre aspects.

Having reached the limit of her patience with Tenoch's and Julio's immature shenanigans and hypocrisy, Luisa exits the journey. That Julio physically pushes her and erupts at her to 'stay out of' his fight with Tenoch signals a turn in the otherwise figurative violence (masculine-specific) in this film. This push revives their earlier objectifications of her at the wedding in physical-material ways, and, if read solely according to classicism, the actions coalesce as theme and social issue like a 'miniature dissertation' on machismo. The film's treatment of these two comparable actions across the narrative, moreover, discloses the social mechanics 'happening with' a larger network of xenochronic-anamorphic comparisons. Meanings build in-between them. Reiteration reveals a crux, one of the points of contact across the film's 'correlational structure,' among very different stages of in-process identity formation (Sobchack 1992: 18–19). These are different for our different characters.

Luisa storms off to find a bus (to popular tourist destination Puerto Escondido, which she had initially suggested and Julio and Tenoch berated in adolescent arrogance as too 'preppy') and complete her trip on her own: 'to hell with you and *your* Heaven's Mouth.' The differences between Luisa's and the adolescents' investments in this trip are manifold. She sarcastically scolds them: 'You're animals! Your manifesto is a bunch of bullshit! You break your own rules.' She admits her own mistakes as countervailing points: 'I'm such an idiot! I thought you'd be different. . . . What the hell was I thinking?' She concludes with a pithy lesson: 'play with babies and you end up washing diapers!'

Two complementary views out the front window center Luisita's stuffed mouse hanging from the rearview mirror graphically overlapping with the image of Luisa walking ahead along the roadside. By association, Luisa aligns more with the vestiges of the late Luisita, Doña Martina, and their family's grave lessons than she does with the adolescents and their failed tests of maturity. Julio and Tenoch remain mostly unaware—of Luisa, themselves, and their surrounding conditions.

Luisa keeps walking away from Tenoch and Julio until they admit their mistakes and negotiate decision-making power. Alongside reasonable frustration, hope re-emerges that lessons might be sinking in. This long take runs 45 seconds, the first 30 seconds in motion up the road right-to-left and the last 15 seconds as Luisa abruptly halts the motion, dropping her bag on the car hood and offering a compromise. Luisa's action punctuates this story-level glitch. Agency circulates around all three (four?) characters, and the long view emphasizes their surrounding environment across the top half of the frame. Luisa restores balance by offering 'my own rules.' Unlike Ceci and Ana who maintain and simply reverse traditional power dynamics, Luisa operates more fairly through mutual exchange with Julio and Tenoch.

Unlike the carnivalesque long take at 'The *Charolastra* Manifesto,' conceptual continuity—a nearly one-minute eight-shot series with convoluted soundtrack—depicts Luisa's manifesto delivery. Her language is noticeably European-Spanish compared tonally and linguistically to so much of the Mexican-Spanish and *Chilango* slang in the 'opposing' manifesto and throughout the film. But the manifestos certainly exceed binary dialectics. The first five shots run in intervals of approximately 5 and 8 seconds, and their directional emphases alternate widely. The continuity is suggested but undercut by a swirl of (mis)direction. More directly, the first seven manifesto items' delivery, voiced by Luisa, favors one rhythm, while the five shots' pacing, at cuts, favor another. Counter-beats are subtly abrasive but generatively perturbing.

By the sixth shot in this series, though, a 12-second view hovers among the three in-car seated characters, mimicking their view out the car of, first, an 'ecotourism' roadside marker and, second, a military roadside inspection. Reiterating the 'stare' at the authorities that earlier shots provided, or even the retrospection on the bricklayer's narrator-identified but unclaimed corpse, this one again pans aside and concludes by gazing upon things our characters avoided and were intimidated to observe, contemplate, and/or challenge. The penultimate 8-second shot of this series again divides the frame in upper and lower halves, with Betsabé and travelers crossing a bridge mid-frame horizontal left-to-right and, below families doing laundry, swimming, and bathing in a river. Background and foreground dialogue but without clear synthesis. A 9-second shot wraps this series with another long exterior anticipatory view as Betsabé approaches from center to lower left. Headlights are now on and the sun hangs low along the horizon. Days lapse over the journey. Things get stranger.

The linearity of the actions both short-cut and short-circuit continuity in this series; spatio-temporal configurations do not match the action as items one through eight enjoy much more daylight than items nine and ten do. Bridging sound elements complicate this achronological logic further. Put directly, the delivery of the manifesto items requiring about a minute of soundtrack spans closer to at least three hours of story time. Location has been, say, progressively ambiguous or at least 'indirect' since the *libre/* liberating exit and pilgrimage encounter. Rather than resolve, this sequence resequences the action, itself diegetically and narratively reiterative, to give credit to the connective limens among the parts in a much greater degree than classical style typically regulates.

The reiterative segments, as a key example those outlined around Luisa's compromise and manifesto delivery, do not stand in binary opposition to associational counterparts but rather invite viewers through a youthful address aware of intimate explorations by the characters to correlate the ideas in a 'strange' dialectic. The poststructural relationships among parts function to expose the narrative, representational modes, identifications, and then, according to xenochronic storytelling more than rationalism, the value-laden social mechanics they emulate. Differences are *differential*.

As *differánce* (unnamed yet neologized) fuses 'different'-*cum*-'deference' in multivalent relationship between structural oppositions for Jacques Derrida's deconstructive function (2008); or, as Sobchack's previously discussed perception-expression 'exchange and reversibility' embodies the cinematic experience among 'correlational' structural elements (1992: 14–19); or, as Barthes' 'third way' pivots in between mythologies' 'hiding nothing' and 'flaunting nothing' to de-structure traditional mythology on the way to something richly 'obtuse' (2012: 240, 232); or, as Žižek's 'shift' enables a background 'stain' to prismatically refract what had previously stood as foreground message (2006a)—(post)structuralist functions often rely on just such contact-for-conversion points. Néstor García Canclini likewise has explained (post)modern 'hybrid transformations' as 'cultural reconversions' whereby multiply-situated 'horizontal coexistence' occurs across 'symbolic systems' (1992: 32).

Building from García Canclini and the idea that dominant-cultural and minoritarian identities access the 'fiction of identity' 'differently' according to engagements with cultural logics, José Esteban Muñoz argues that 'identities-in-difference' can enact a sense of self 'at precisely the point where discourses of essentialism and constructivism short-circuit' one another for 'disidentifications' (1999: 6–9). These all offer ways to imagine the relationships among and 'in-between' the parts of *Tu Mamá*'s strange dialectics and identity processes. Especially applicable to Luisa and her manifesto, Chela Sandoval theorizes transformative identity formations, sometimes framed as *mestiza*-Latina and contextualized around third world feminisms but certainly not limited by those contexts, according to a 'differential consciousness' (2000).

Differential consciousness figures as both 'process and shifting location' outside of discursive referentiality (*ibid.*: 140, 6). Sandoval aligns it with Gloria Anzaldúa's 'workings of the "soul"' and Audre Lorde's 'mobile "erotic" as a place where our "our deepest knowledges" are found' (*ibid.*: 6). Sandoval re-reads later Barthes, especially *A Lover's Discourse* (1978), to

help explain the operation of the alternative-to-dominant consciousness.
Citing Barthes, Sandoval adduces that differential consciousness "'can only
be reached" by human thought through an unconformable and "intractable"
passage—not through any "synthetic term"—but rather through another
kind of "eccentric" and "extraordinary"' 'conduit' (2000 139; cf. Barthes
1978: 55). Revolutionary love takes bountiful forms.

Sandoval elaborates that eccentricities vary 'from revolt to religious
experience, from *rasquache* to punk,' which recasts several notable environments depicted in *Tu Mamá*—Tenoch, Leo, and Our Lady in the Iturbide
family room; Saba's mixed-style post-punk neo-hippy apartment; Luisa and
Jano's academic-cluttered apartment; Doña Martina's *ofrenda*/altar; and
elsewhere. Further, Sandoval borrows Barthes's 'conduit' as a 'punctum,'
comparable to a glitch, a pointed rupture in a dominant symbolic system
that de-natures it and allows access through it to an alternate set of procedures; the most crucial irruption is revolutionary love (2000: 139–40).

The effect of falling in love and the language of lovers—experience
alongside expression-perception—disrupt 'everyday narratives that tie us
to social time and space, to the descriptions, recitals, and plots that dull and
order our senses' and, as a result, open up to an otherwise impossible 'place
of possibility' (*ibid.*: 141). This anything-is-possible 'unlimited space' provides 'meanings unanchored and moving away from their traditional moor-
ings,' comparable to primordial considerations (*ibid.*). A crucial facet of
*Tu Mamá*'s youthful address, revolutionary love modulates revolutionary
hermeneutics and *movidas* (survival strategies) particularly for those traditionally appropriated (conventionalized) and dispossessed (exiled) by
dominant-hegemonic models (*ibid.*).

Luisa as *la Madrileña* reiterates—updates and permutates—and compos-
itely refigures competing notions of Spanish Conquest and its effects on
Mexican (mythic) nationalism. Luisa's character complicates references to
conqueror (Cortés), *la Malinche* (Doña Marina, punning in some ways with
Doña Martina), and *Hija de la Chingada* as mestiza daughter born of their
union (and the invocation of existential labyrinths of solitude, generations
of cosmic races, and combinations thereof).[1] She hides and flaunts nothing.
Luisa exists outside of any one of these instances through her revolutionary
love, yet her now-living material form remains trapped amid competing
realities concretely present, historically constructed, as well as imagined.

Sandoval's revolutionary love combines freedoms and joys (Barthes's
famous *jouissance*) with death and uncertainty: when one is engulfed in
love, meanings in the 'abyss' 'emerg[e] to haunt all we think we know'
(*ibid.*). The 'dispersed lover' is equally a 'traveler' making a 'painful crossing to this no-place, this chiasmus, this crossroads' but without clear direction or material destination: the 'trans-forming lover' ultimately 'drifts'

beyond any partnerships and life-death status but is free of ideology and social structure in a differential consciousness triggered by revolution-love (*ibid.*). These are ever-becoming processes.

It is tempting to consider the sex scenes throughout *Tu Mamá* in directly comparative terms and with some matching-action logic. Same goes for Luisa's phone calls with Jano; swimming contests; trips to the country club; etc. But more crucial is the differential consciousness invited by the film's youthful address of revolutionary love and across a network of ideas associated with intimacy. *Tu Mamá*'s reiterative climaxes exemplify this.

Inaccessible by car and road, guided by Chuy's family, and transported by boat across water, our trio finally arrives at Boca del Cielo. They enjoy the diversions. They then return to find their camp infested by wild pigs—the ever-returning savage state in our course of empires. Our trio takes Chuy's offer of a beachside cabana and a welcome cold shower. Before retiring, Julio and Tenoch challenge one another in games while Luisa makes a final call to Jano. *Mise-en-scène* depicts this as quasi split screen: a window reflection on left shows the adolescents playing foosball, while on right Luisa sits inside another public telephone booth talking with Jano, now returned to Mexico City from his conference. Although his voice is absent, this conversation treated in a 128-second long take begins by compromising with Jano's values—that Luisa's actions are not out of 'revenge' and that neither is to 'blame' nor 'hate' the other. Luisa also deflects Jano's concerns of what his mother will think of their separation.

As viewers come to understand Luisa's condition, Jano's values seem puerile and selfish. By conversation's end, Luisa successfully delivers on her aim to share her intimate thoughts and lessons with Jano: namely, she instructs him to 'learn to be happy' as she has even facing death. Whether Jano applies the lessons going forward remains doubtful, yet the point is in Luisa's affirmative delivery and the film's usefully unanswered questions. Both calls end with '*cuídate,*' 'take care of yourself,' as she submits a 'tender' farewell. At the moment she hangs up, she weeps but redirects her concerns to Julio and Tenoch, just as they shout out in excitement over their competitive, trifling games.

Luisa's incremental expressions of intimacy since joining this road trip set the stage for the sexual event that involves the three of them. An astounding 416-second shot follows Luisa left-to-right to a beachside table where the trio has drinks. The first 336 seconds depict their conversation, filling in selective gaps that were previously left vacant as partial truths and half-lies. The hand-held shot is book-ended by conventional establishing shots that situate this conversation in the larger environment, and during this conversation our trio makes frequent digressions to a neighboring table. The shot shifts in and out of slightly oblique angle as the conversation extends refinements of sexual techniques gradually disclosed throughout their travels; Julio and Tenoch admit even greater indiscretions and infidelity with each other's girlfriends; and Luisa affirms them as 'cool dudes' and Mexico as a 'magical, musical' place. Tenoch's and Julio's reconciliation barely accommodates traditional class-based values, momentarily reinstalling a *Charolastra* stamp on their friendship.

The final 80 seconds of this shot again follow Luisa as she picks a song on the jukebox and then dances a direct-address into the camera, refocusing critical attention to instruments of revolutionary love. With each affirmation, the group toasts, celebrates, and drinks. A note of forgiveness draws our trio closer together, with Julio's sincere apology to Luisa meeting '*un beso*,' a 'kiss' to seal their agreements. This narrative event partially fulfills our climax, but reiterative climaxes continue.

This kiss is reiterated in the following 127-second shot, as the trio engages in a *ménage-a-trois*. Again the hand-held camera as multiply-identifying embodiment 'walks' into the action, sliding occasionally oblique. It does not advantage any single character's perspective nor fully objective vantage but instead shows the group's shared intimacy. The filmmakers and cast claimed they 'approached the sex scenes like all the others,' with sex being 'only a result' of an honest moment of sharing among the characters (Cuarón quoted in Basoli 2002: 28). The director explained that the production never tried to capture the 'nice cinematic moment or the postcard location' (*ibid.*). After brainstorming ideas for lighting this climactic scene, the filmmakers decided that candlelight was 'too cute' but that a single light bulb avoided glamorizing or romanticizing the sexuality (Cuarón quoted in Pulver 2013). Stylistic exigencies recover primordial meanings in this honest moment. This sex scene most fully accumulates the processes of questioning and transformation from the previous intimate scenes.

Group sex, actual and imaginary, has built up questions of identification throughout this story, and the *ménage-a-trois* explores the questions in concentrated detail. Moreover, as love and intimacy are explored, the long-take cinematography—and the larger resequencing with conceptual continuity surrounding the actions—discloses not just its representation but its structurally determined representative values. This *ménage à trois*— sexual threesome in the vernacular but also literally three-part 'household' management and economic 'ecology'—merges value systems in order to complicate and test their identity-based questions. Nudity symbolizes disclosures. Each 'loving, passionate kiss,' '*beso jugoso, de amor*' offers the fullest expression of shared intimacy among our trio.

Alfonso Cuarón directly refutes the suggestion that this scene's emphasis is a homosexual initiation for Tenoch and Julio: the story 'is not about homosexuality, not the story of two gay men coming out of the closet' (quoted in

Fernández 2001). Worse, an isolated queer reading of this scene likely leads to an interpretation of the next-morning reactions as revulsion for same-sex identifications and a mark of homophobia. That these values coexist among the competing realities around the film must be acknowledged. To the extent this issue is available to our reading, the youthful address repositions it among the film's conceptual patterns and de-structured network of ideas.

This *ménage-a-trois* reveals a physical union among Luisa, Julio, and Tenoch that comes as close as this story will to fulfilling the possibilities of transforming their intimacy. Love and sex here, as Cuarón explains, show Julio's and Tenoch's similar nature but prove their intractable differences and immaturity compared to Luisa (*ibid.*). Their morning-after dread corresponds to their inability to escape the social condition that has held them in place (*ibid.*) Youthful sexuality, especially articulated through reiterative manifestos, differentiates their 'being' *contra* 'becoming.'

The sex scenes as well as the manifestos, all in a reiterative manner and with differential consciousness in transaction, affirmed bonds among the characters that, voice-over narration anticipated earlier, create a solid indivisibility. The universe of stories is adorned by mythologies. They reveal truths as partial. They all three continue to break their own rules; they ignore or deny their complicated conditions. Like Julio and Tenoch, viewers continue twisting the details to complete the puzzle of this narrative. Only more painful truths await—obvious but all the more difficult to accept.

## Note

1. Regarding character naming, see Acevedo-Muñoz (2004: 40–1), Saldaña-Portillo (2005: 760–1, 767), and Lahr-Vivaz (2006: 83–4).

# 10 Ecstasy

An epilogue, the closing 197 seconds of the film consisting of 12 shots, advances *Tu Mamá*'s timeline to the end of the summer the year after the beach trip. Viewers recognize that PRI, 'the ruling party' in Mexico for the last 71 years, lost the national presidency to PAN-nominee Vicente Fox. This shift in governance, regardless of actual political values and cultural nationalism involved, strikes an unresolved chord like Godard's mid-1960s France, Luisa's girlhood post-Franco Spain, even the contemporized-historical Benito Juárez mural passed during travel through Oaxaca. How much change can one expect from social-political revolutions, one must consider? How are these instituted through constitutions, reforms, manifestos, and the like? How much real good can one movie do?

*Tu Mamá* does much—less in answers and more in refining how and why we ask questions. Alfonso Cuarón suggests that Fox and PAN did not win but rather PRI lost, and the struggle for a 'mature' Mexican democracy is 'day by day' and ongoing (quoted in Feinstein 2002). *Tu Mamá*'s dialectics end not in synthesis but in coming-to-be processes and yet-to-be-fully-answered questioning. Mythologies of youth disclose the structures and raise up for examination the values they maintain. Mexico's turn-of-the-century social condition witnesses competing realities that coincide but do not recognize one another, and these encumber incongruities among traditional values in identity construction across class, gender, sexual orientation, ethnicity, citizenship, and more.

In this closing sequence viewers also learn that Julio and Tenoch have been apart since they returned from their trip. The familiar, diegetically tangential narrator delivers this information in the 26th voice-over entry with some sense of irony since precise timing shows the two running into each other by happenstance on a busy downtown Mexico City street [see Figure 10.1]. That they have 'stopped seeing each other' yet now literally *see each other* opens the epilogue. Concluding the epilogue and film, Julio lightly offers 'see you around?,' Tenoch replies noncommittally 'sure,' while the narrator forecloses on possibilities: 'they will never meet again.'

*Figure 10.1* Shoplifters of the World Uniting; or, *Charolastras'* Chance Meeting?

Contradictions beg explanation in this closing sequence. Not 'seeing each other' empathically and ignoring each other's mundane realities in spite of it being right in front of them amounts to a Mexican-millennial condition, even (especially?) when it is as obvious as the surrounding cityscape.

They greet one another with an adult handshake, recalling the ceremonial greetings throughout the story. A conventional establishing shot is nuanced as a long-take of 45-second duration; rather than 'established' in this new setting, Julio and Tenoch are diminished by the busy *mise-en-scène*. Hand-held but steadier than the majority of shots throughout this film, the long view depicts an actual intersection—cars, police, and pedestrian traffic running almost entirely right-to-left one-way and skyscrapers block the left and right. Signs point to this world of global commerce, state regulation, traditional privilege, and modern social order—Pepsi advertisement, a bank sign, street lights, high-fashion marketing, and commerce. Like several of our voice-over entries, diegetic sounds of the horseback police, car horns and traffic, and city sounds in general chaotically underlie the narrator's delivery. Tenoch arrives from right with a Tower Records purchase in one hand and meets Julio, one of the few visual weights moving left-to-right, just a few steps off the curb. Both sport much 'preppier' wardrobe and hair-styles than just over a year earlier. They are becoming what they earlier disdained. First in graphic collision, they join, merge with traffic again, and go for a cup of coffee, which the narrator judges and shares 'was less awkward than making excuses to avoid it.'

The concluding 11 shots are interior of a Wings diner, where Julio and Tenoch sit in a booth and catch up with one another. The soundtrack favors their dialogue but muted city sounds from just outside their window and around the restaurant incessantly interrupt it. The narrator overviews that Ceci and Ana broke up with them after their return from Europe; two months later Tenoch started dating a female neighbor; and nine months later Julio started dating a girl from French class. Whatever tension over same-sex relationships exists for either Julio or Tenoch or both after their homosexual kiss and *ménage-a-trois* with Luisa matches with acceptance of their gay friend Daniel's 'total queen' lifestyle because he 'got a boyfriend and everything' and 'he's super happy.' They equally find that 'his dad kicked him out' reprehensible. It would be difficult to read their deportments as homophobic per se or even sexually repressed in traditional terms. But clearly they struggle with sharing intimacy.

They also are not keeping up with Saba, who has moved away. Pecas goes entirely unmentioned. The *Charolastras* have traveled in different directions into adulthood. If their earlier debates concluded with 'hot chicks,' this conversation remains even shallower with things being 'cool,' 'good,' or 'that sucks,' and the dialogue is soft-spoken and appropriate for the setting. Julio and Tenoch mostly conform to their circumstances. Tension does exist for Julio and Tenoch, now in their twenties, adolescence in their rearview mirror, and days away from starting college. Julio will study biology at the metropolitan public university UAM. Tenoch will attend ITAM, the private university known for its prestigious business school, in his father-approved economics (Julio conjectures correctly) rather than his stated preference in literature.

In a rare departure from the long takes and stylized montage from the rest of the film, these last 11 shots feature a series of medium-size shot-countershots in fairly quick pace that relatively conventionally depicts the disclosure of Luisa's ailment and death to cancer just a month after Julio and Tenoch returned to Mexico City. Unlike conceptual continuity characteristic of the film, which situates characters within their environment and yields transidentifications, these diner shots are more fully subjective and focalize the information about Luisa's death through Julio's and Tenoch's young-adult perspectives and learning processes. Conventional manners benefit from conventional forms. Luisa's decision to keep her illness a secret amplifies for Julio and Tenoch that her hope was to use what time she had left in her life to grow and to help them grow during their trip together. Luisa dedicated her life to sacrifice, and in her most mature incarnation she exhibits the virtues of selflessness. Julio and Tenoch exhibit compassion for her loss, and their chagrin predominantly owes to their own inabilities to learn from her and the group experiences together.

Alfonso Cuarón claims that the difficulties Julio and Tenoch have in defining their identities ultimately 'is their biggest conflict' (quoted in Basoli 2002: 28). The *ménage-a-trois* climax reveals that they are 'very similar' characters, 'essentially the same' as young adults and, according to the director, 'what keeps them separate is the social conditioning':

> When they start finding out their true identity, that they are so similar, they get so scared that they have to seek shelter in some mask. The tragedy at the end is that the mask is the social conditioning they were trying to escape from at the beginning.
>
> (*ibid.*)

That our adolescent characters correlate with Mexico's upper and middle classes who 'live in a bubble' and 'travel through Mexico and still not connect with what is going on around them' suggests an equally tragic moment for millennial Mexico and the world (*ibid.*: 26–27).

Mainly what remains unsaid between Julio and Tenoch at the film's end, then, is their growing awareness that they have failed to outsmart the adult world (as they suggested they would during the wedding), that they have lost their youthful spirit of revolutionary 'becoming,' and that they have succumbed to the blandly oppressive social conditions of the 21st century (as many viewers must realize we all have too). Julio (and the middle classes) 'insisted on paying the check,' and Tenoch and his girlfriend (and the upper classes) 'go to the movies.' If the epilogue leaves us a bit depressed or dissatisfied by the un-'happy ending,' we might review the hopeful questions Act Three raises through Luisa's transformations.

*Tu Mamá*'s adolescent characters sometimes at parties take ecstasy. A late-20th-century generational signature 'club drug,' ecstasy is a psychoactive drug used recreationally to incite feelings of hallucinogenic euphoria, distortions of time and disorientations in space, increased empathy and trust, heightened sensations of sexual energy, and reduced inhibitions. Note, first, that empathy, trust, and intimacy represent values being tested for the characters as they consider their in-formation and in-crisis identities. Second, the *Lover's Discourse* frequently associates love and lover's language as drug-like in its effects, which fold into differential consciousness (Barthes 1978: 60–1; Sandoval 2000: 144–7). Third, Saba's altered/experimental state of mind provided this journey direction from start.

To be clear, drug use is not a key issue per se but its associational qualities are transformative and conventionally provocative. 'Ecstatic' side effects link in several respects to the experimental qualities of narration: the Cuarón brand of cinema language exceeds the sober efficiencies of storytelling through alternating sequencing and xenochronic continuity. On the one hand, finding any respite from constraints can feel intoxicatingly liberating even if (especially if) jumbled, divergent, and out-of-step with normality. More profoundly, healthier and even spiritually informed notions of ecstasy reside in the opportunities for multiply complex identifications throughout this narrative and especially at the destination of our characters' road trip. Functionally, Boca del Cielo opens a corridor from our world into another place, a fantastic environment. Arrival there embodies 'a paradise on earth.' A threshold to 'heaven' displaces the binary of life-afterlife.

The *Charolastras* invent this concept/place out of a hope they seem to abandon by story's end. Luisa adopts the concept most fully. Viewers fairly recognize the impracticality or irony of this 'new world order' arising in a character fatally ill. But Alfonso Cuarón claims that, facing death in the end of our story, Luisa is 'ecstatic' (quoted in Fernández 2001). Her profound joy ascribes to the idea of discovering a new order through the processes of becoming. Having tried but recognized her failure at offering Tenoch and Julio transformational intimacy and the possibility to experiment with confluent love, Luisa compromises with her own manifesto to deal with them. Yet she continues exploring and displaying her own transformations of consciousness. A few miles down the road a few hours later, Julio and Tenoch turn off the main road to a dirt road miraculously like the one Saba foretold. Night falls on them with one wheel stuck in the sand, and Act Two closes. Again the plot point is reiterative.

'Julio and Tenoch clearly had no idea where they were or how to get somewhere they'd never been,' the 20th voice-over entry explains. Part of this makes sense because 'Saba's directions contradicted each another,' and even before the trip the two acknowledge their mythic destination '*no existe*,' simply 'does not exist.' They also remain lost in their own identities-in-transition from adolescence to adulthood, especially in the crucible of intimacy provided by Luisa. Allegorically, this makes equal sense as their in-formation identities parallel cultural changes throughout Mexico and the world at the threshold of a new century. Their feelings are described as fear by the narrator but of being discovered inadequate for what the future holds. They have glimpsed an ever-becoming future and have two words: go back.

Luisa, the narrator's next voice-over entry will disclose, also remains struck by a fear that 'kept her awake' but 'had nothing to do with the darkness or surroundings,' about which Julio and Tenoch remain ignorant and she chooses not to share. A new day dawned, and by some strange miracle Betsabé has traveled a dirt path that gives way to the Pacific Ocean. Like at a slit in time, Act Two comes-to-be Act Three having finally arrived at a beach (the beach? a mythic beach?). The Cuaróns' screenplay calls for a 'fade out/fade in' curtain effect at this moment, which does not appear in the film (2001: 195). Instead, even more fully in keeping with the Cuarón brand of language, a xenochronic inversion depicts Luisa feigning sleep the night before that transforms to Luisa waking the next morning.

The night-time shot from just outside the car window reveals Luisa cast in darkness and shadows and bedded down in the backseat [see Figure 10.2]. The medium shot shows her body at a diagonal-right from the lower-left corner of the frame to center with the right half of the frame filled with Betsabé's intersecting lines. The image initially echoes Luisa's similar instances of repose, the most proximate aligning her with the funeral procession the group passes after car repairs, and she opens her eyes and stares into a vacant distance. Cricket chirps convert to birdsong at the cut. In the corresponding morning shot, the camera 'sits' alongside her in the backseat streaked by sunlight [see Figure 10.3]. This fuller shot reveals her knees-up at a diagonal-left along the body of the frame and rising to top-left corner of the frame. Imagery collisions at this inter-act invite xenochrony. Again her eyes open, squint into the brightness, and go in search of the new day in this fantastic place. Plot-point 'arrivals' overlap reiteratively across this catalog of shots; the style exceeds efficient storytelling yet remains accessible.

Extending from a fear/woke strange dialectic, a seemingly linear-causal relationship in the following three shots totaling 65 seconds suggests Luisa exits the car and walks along the beach destination. Thoroughly 'transitional,' a rich multivalence of 'awakening' invites viewers to consider supplementary interpretations. These opening three shots of Act Three are long views that resituate Luisa in this atopic non-place or heterotopic fantasy-space where things can be *different*. A 16-second long take reveals her emerging, stretching skyward, and reshaping herself for this new existence. After a slight stumble, she leaves Betsabé behind and strides forward with shoulders broad and arms wide, almost flying through this space. She

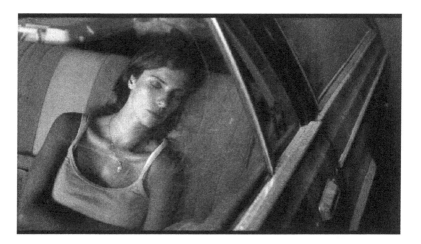

*Figure 10.2* Nighttime Xenochronically Becoming Daytime: Luisa Fearful, Asleep . . .

*Figure 10.3* . . . Then 'Woke'

takes everything in. A 25-second long take follows with the first 10 seconds anticipatory of her walking into the 'standing' eye-level camera and then pausing to scan the horizon ahead, which is not answered by the conventional eye-line match. Instead, the shot holds on her 'becoming' in this new environment and progresses another 15 seconds as an awed Luisa is first stunned and then enraptured by the beach disappearing into ocean depth. She runs down a sandy embankment and toward a rocky outcropping that reshapes the horizon.

Just as the visuals are multi-directional, the soundtrack layers her metronomic footsteps with organic whirls of sea breeze and crashing waves against bird chirps. The sequence offers several formal textures as access points to the experience rather than seamless continuity-based linearity. She removes her shoes and begins a gradual shedding of material artifacts that will continue through the remainder of the story. Barefoot she wades in the surf converging at her feet seeming to arrive in waves from different directions at once. Tenoch's premonition at the wedding comes true: 'heaven turns into the sea.' Akin to Emerson's 'transparent eyeball,' Luisa absorbs her new environment and the camera mimics her—seeing all, being nothing, but coming-to-be the currents of Universal Being that circulate around and through them (2003: 39). Luisa's actions can be considered in superficial terms, but this Act Three threshold invites multiply ambivalent identifications with character and character-in-environment in a revolutionary condition.

Is this 'the' Boca del Cielo? Viewers discover, no, that arrival is enabled and named as such by Chuy and his family—accessible by boat, it seems. But is it *una boca del cielo*, a passageway to Luisa's next plane of existence? Is it the gates of heaven? Nirvana? Is she reincarnated? Is this a purgatory where she purifies herself after having confronted her sins and been forgiven in preparation for entering the eternal joy of after-life? Has the film inched along through gradual disclosures of intimacy in stuttering stops and starts only to land here? I argue that this film provides viewers inciting questions without clear answers. *Tu Mamá* provides 'ways of reacting to things' and opportunities to reposition, look again, and think differently. Furthermore, this may come as close as *Tu Mamá* does at consolidating the isolated readings throughout the film. Values arise across the network traces, and the benefit, nevertheless, remains in the acts of questioning, in sheer possibilities surrounding transformative processes of becoming. Precisely without the answers, without structural delimitations, questions embody our daily routines but also ascend to eschatology and the ever-after-becoming.

While camping at the beach, Julio, Tenoch, and Luisa enjoy some time apart. Anyone traveling with others in a cramped car on a road trip will not be surprised. But their divorcement and seeking solitude probably more directly correlates with the failures of their tests of identity formation—adolescent in-formation for Julio and Tenoch and in-crisis for ailing Luisa. Julio and Tenoch, especially after prompting by Chuy, eventually swim, manage camp, and play *fútbol* together. They even play make-believe national star ballers with Chuy's narration.

Luisa integrates into Chuy's and Mabel's family, drawn especially to their daughter Lucero through an association to Doña Martina and her granddaughter Luisita. Luisa undergoes the fullest transformation of any character in *Tu Mamá*, most directly evidenced in her redefined sense of community/family. Once they actually arrive at the beach known as Boca del Cielo proper, Luisa swims with Lucero, but their game is to 'float like a corpse.' Luisa professes: Lucero is 'teaching me how to swim,' child instructing the adult, and a quick underwater shot removes their bodied existence from the rest of the social condition like a temporary death. Xenochrony draws associations from this swimming lesson backward to earlier swimming races and forward to Luisa's soon arrival into the surf. This make-believe game of 'corpse,' ironically ecstatic about death, situates Luisa's 'ever-becoming' engagements with her new surrogate family. As much as for Marcelino Escutia, remembrances matter. As much as for Doña Martina, love approaches revolution. Idyllic dreams crash as waves roll with tides: Luisa's cancer persists, and Chuy and Mabel lose their livelihood, lifestyle, and family legacy in corporate fell swoops.

Toward the end of their day at Boca del Cielo, our trio finally does reunite, sitting together in the sand, smoking marijuana, and gazing at the ocean horizon. 'You ever wish you could live forever?,' Luisa thoughtfully propositions Tenoch and Julio, who reply with simplistic 'sure' and 'totally.' Luisa tries again here, and reiteratively over drinks and at the cabana that night, to share intimacy with the adolescents who continue to fail their adult tests. She delivers her final attempt at confluent love with them in something of a riddle they (and viewers) will need to contemplate for years to come.

While Julio and Tenoch struggle with manual chores of packing, Luisa strolls down the beach and finds a pleasant swimming spot. She is depicted in a medium shot that sequences with a first-person subjective shot as she peers back up the shoreline to the adolescents. The long view anchors a highly imbalanced shot-countershot. Even more so than similar long shots with the sun hanging low in the sky at sunset or early-morning sunrise, this view de-emphasizes the significance of any one individual life and 're-establishes' the larger lessons for viewers grounded by classical paradigm readings to reconsider—nothing new under the sun.

These are truly existential, cathartic, and eschatological considerations. A 25-second long take concludes Act Three [see Figure 10.4]. As Luisa again wades through the surf and plunges into the ocean depth, the camera follows behind and briefly underwater for viewers to observe and swim vicariously. Precisely because we have no clear resolution, no absolute synthesis of ideas, the discourse abstracts into life-ever-after marveling. What are our reasons for being—and ever-becoming? Head and arms at water's surface, body submerged, Luisa surrenders joyfully, ecstatically, into the (super) natural of this fantastic environment. The 25th voice-over entry consecrates Luisa's last words to Julio and Tenoch: '*La vida es como la espuma. Por eso*

*Figure 10.4* Transubstantiating Luisa in Sea-Becoming-Heaven

*hay que darse como el mar,*' 'Life is like the foam, so give yourself away like the sea.'

The story of *Y Tu Mamá También* offers this mythologized story of youthful transition, not only for our teenage Julio and Tenoch approaching adulthood or only for the in-formation social groups like Mexico at the turn to the 21st century. Even in her tragic end, Luisa's hopefulness buoys possibilities for revolutionary transformation.

# 11  *Pranganeando*

Viewers returning to *Y Tu Mamá También* may be shocked (shocked to their systems) at its prescience. Over the first two decades of the 21st century since its release, information exchanges lost in between subjectivity—with its individual insights, convictions, and biases—and objectivity—with its impartiality, empirical discipline, but false hope of absolute truth—have swirled around determinations of 'fact.' Sometimes an odd detail helps redirect and refocus our attention to something truer in the whole. Sometimes we arrive at intuitive revelations by miracle, accident, or willed nonconformity. Sometimes a movie puzzles us to ask inciting questions. Art can entertain us by revealing our divided realities and lend us perspective to see through and above them. We cross thresholds in pursuit of greater understanding. But how often have we met misinformation, disinformation, false accounts, some of which confirm our hopes, false beliefs, and partial truths, only to not check their force? Worse, how do these agglomerate contradictory realities around a divided world? We get stuck at intersections.

Propaganda and yellow journalism are certainly not new, but our so-called 'post-truth' uses of information sciences and technologies like internet-based communication and social media have made these global pathways, as Thomas Friedman famously augurs, flatter, faster, and more crowded (2008). *Tu Mamá* is not 'about' the Obama U.S. presidency, the Trump U.S. presidency, Brexit, deforestation in South America, nor the López Obrador Mexican presidency any more than it is 'about' the PRI-PAN transition nor any other isolated and singular issue. And yet its millennial lessons address many of these at their core and across their 'wilder' networks. *Tu Mamá* delivers 'ways of reacting to things,' to look at things again differently, strangely. Mythologies expose their structures; adolescence affords profound transformations of their values.

One manner in which contemporary youth movies are growing more dynamic, complex, and revealing is through treatments of science and technology, especially around information exchanges (Shary 2002: 209, 210,

264). Stereotypically the province of the 'geeks,' mastery over science and technology in thematic terms affords youthful heroes an opportunity for renewed social acceptance and demonstrations of maturity and sophistication (*ibid.*: 202). Differences between Western and non-Western films certainly figure alongside cultural expressions and 'digital divides.'

In *Tu Mamá* technology appears but appears vaguely retrogressive. Communication is clearly not the mark of heroism for Tenoch and Julio. Our characters communicate by landline telephones, some even in decrepit public payphone booths. Mobile telephony and internet cultures emerging by the late-1990s in Western cultures seem altogether nonexistent in *Tu Mamá's fin-de-siècle* world. Glitches disturb storylines and social mechanics more often than high-tech operations. Our characters are not early adopters of the social media wave. Our characters listen to and own CDs for music. Ceci's newer, more expensive personal computer in her bedroom exemplifies her and her family's privilege compared to the disadvantages suggested by the shared 'classic' Macintosh stationed in Julio's family room. Likewise, Julio and his sister must share a handed-down Betsabé while Tenoch takes for granted his 'Batmobile,' a new model, imported Jetta graduation present. Generally, Mexico City scenes appear bustling, industrial-mechanical, and not particularly new-age digital, and travel south gradually decreases the amount but not the impact of modernity's technologies.

*Tu Mamá*'s script offers some insight to our *Charolastras*: '*se volvieron una familia del desmadre, unidos para pranganear por el mundo*' (Cuarón and Cuarón 2001: 31). The richly ambiguous slang best translates 'they formed a family out of a fucked-up situation, united to [*pranganear*] around the world.' '*Pranganeando*' particularly resists easy translation and factors variously: partying, scrounging, punking, pranking, supertramping, and above all refusing to conform. It aspires to a perfect combination of lazing about, adventurous experience, and independence. This yields particular sympathy with the *Charolastras*' desperation and precarious immaturity, but it also suggests their hope and, for Julio and Tenoch in the café at story's end, delineates their failure. They merge into traffic, they follow their directed pathways however imbalanced they appear, and they go *forward* . . . to college and beyond. They avert their attention from where our camera repeatedly aims to challenge authority. They settle into expected roles. They conform. The more things change, the more they reiterate.

Technology, communication, science, and positivism surround our characters' journey as stylized modes. Luisa's communication frequently participates in the materially grounded forms of technology but also communes with and conveys higher-order existential lessons. Although rarely explicitly part of their conversation, what seems practically always at stake for our characters is their maturity, their capability to interact and process information in humane ways, and the structures that deliver these. *Tu Mamá* offers a journey of discovery. It is not 'about' youth as much as it offers youthful 'ways of reacting to things.' It points out divorcements and faults and structured circumstances underlying them. However limited its *denouements*, its reiterative conflicts and climaxes are entertaining and revelatory. Its strange logic and conceptual continuity only draw loose associations around mythologies surrounding youthfulness, and yet its complex (post) structural forms invite all of us into experiential processes of becoming. We find keys in asking provocative, meaningful questions.

# Bibliography

Acevedo-Muñoz, E. (2004) 'Sex, Class, and Mexico in Alfonso Cuarón's *Y Tu Mamá También*,' *Film & History*, 34.1, pp 39–48.

Anhelo (2002) *Production Notes*, online, <http://cinema.com/articles/812/> [accessed December 2018].

Atkinson, M. (1994) 'Crossing the Frontiers,' *Sight and Sound*, 4.1, pp 14–17.

Aufderheide, P. (2001) 'Review,' *Cineaste*, 27.1, pp 32–3.

Barthes, R. (1978) *A Lover's Discourse: Fragments*, New York: Hill and Wang (translated by R. Howard).

Barthes, R. (2012 [1957]) *Mythologies*, New York: Hill and Wang (translated by R. Howard and A. Lavers).

Basoli, A. (2002) 'Interview,' *Cineaste*, 27.3, pp 26–9.

Baugh, S. (2004a) 'Developing History/Historicizing Development in Mexican *Nuevo Cine* Manifestoes around "*la Crisis*",' *Film & History*, 34.2, pp 25–37.

Baugh, S. (2004b) 'Manifesting *la Historia*: Systems of "Development" and the New Latin American Cinema Manifestoes,' *Film & History*, 34.1, pp 56–65.

Belsey, C. (2002) *Poststucturalism*, Oxford: Oxford University Press.

Benjamin, W. (1998 [1934]) *Understanding Brecht*, London: Verso (translated by A. Bostock).

Benson-Allott, C. (2009) 'Sex Versus the Small Screen,' *Jump Cut*, online, 51, <www.ejumpcut.org/archive/jc51.2009/tuMamaTambien/index> [accessed December 2018].

Bordwell, D. (1985) *Narration in the Fiction Film*, Madison: University of Wisconsin Press.

Bordwell, D. (2006) *The Way Hollywood Tells It: Story and Style in Modern Movies*, Berkeley: University of California Press.

Branigan, E. (1992) *Narrative Comprehension and Film*, New York: Routledge.

Brody, R. (2008) *Everything Is Cinema: The Working Life of Jean-Luc Godard*, New York: Holt.

Caro, M. (2002) 'Review,' *Chicago Tribune*, online, 5 April, <www.chicagotribune.com/news/ct-xpm-2002-04-05-0204050303-story.html> [accessed December 2018].

Carr, P. (2013a) 'Introduction' in Carr, P. (ed) *Frank Zappa and the And*, Farnham: Ashgate, pp 1–15.

Carr, P. (2013b) 'Zappa and Technology,' in Carr, P. (ed) *Frank Zappa and the And*, Farnham: Ashgate, pp 133–47.

Cohan, S., and Hark, I. (1997) *The Road Movie Book*, New York: Routledge.

Considine, D. (1985) *The Cinema of Adolescence*, Jefferson: McFarland.

Corrigan, T. (1991) *A Cinema Without Walls: Movies and Culture After Vietnam*, New Brunswick: Rutgers University Press.

Cuarón, A. (2007) 'Film-Makers Without Borders,' *The Guardian*, online, 5 February, <www.theguardian.com/film/filmblog/2007/feb/05/makingmovieswithoutborders> [accessed December 2018].

Cuarón, C., and Cuarón, A. (2001) *Y Tu Mamá También: Guión y Argumento Cinematográfico*, Mexico City: Anhelo.

Cubitt, S. (2017) 'Glitch,' *Cultural Politics*, 13.1, pp 19–33.

Daix, P. (1966) 'Interview,' *Les Lettres Françaisis*, 121, p 17.

Davis, N. (2014) 'I Love You, *Hombre*,' in DeAngelis, M. (ed) *Reading the Bromance: Homosocial Relationships in Film and Television*, Detroit: Wayne State University Press, pp 109–38.

Derrida, J. (2008 [1968]) '*Differánce*,' in Badminton, N., and Thomas, J. (eds) *Routledge Critical and Cultural Theory Reader*, New York: Routledge, pp 126–48.

Díaz, R. (2005) 'El viaje como desintegración y fundación ideological,' *Ciberletras*, online, 13, <www.lehman.cuny.edu/ciberletras/v13/diaz.htm> [accessed December 2018].

Durbin, K. (2002) 'Review,' *New York Times*, online, 17 March, <www.nytimes.com/2002/03/17/movies/film-comedy-of-a-sexual-provocateur.html?scp=21&st=nyt> [accessed December 2018].

Elsaesser, T., and Buckland, W. (2002) *Studying Contemporary American Film*, London: Arnold.

Emerson, R. (2003 [1836]) *Nature and Selected Essays*, New York: Penguin.

Feinstein, H. (2002) 'Mexican Rave,' *The Guardian*, online, 10 April, <www.theguardian.com/culture/2002/apr/10/artsfeatures> [accessed December 2018].

Fernández, J. (2001) 'Interview,' *Revista Pantella*, online, 12 September, <www.revistapantalla.com/telemundo/entrevistas/?id_nota=414> [accessed December 2018].

Finnegan, N. (2007) 'So What's Mexico Really Like?' in Shaw, D. (ed) *Contemporary Latin American Cinema: Breaking Into the Global*, Lanham: Rowman and Littlefield, pp 29–50.

Friedman, T. (2008) *Hot, Flat, and Crowded*, New York: Farrar.

Galloway, S. (2007) 'Interview,' *The Hollywood Reporter*, online, 12 March, <www.hollywoodreporter.com/news/dialogue-alfonso-cuaron-131782> [accessed December 2018].

Galloway, S. (2014) 'Interview,' *The Hollywood Reporter*, online, 18 February, <www.hollywoodreporter.com/news/alfonso-cuaron-how-angelina-jolie-681003> [accessed December 2018].

García Canclini, N. (1992) *Transforming Modernity: Popular Culture in Mexico*, Austin: University of Texas Press (translated by L. Lozano).

García Tsao, L. (2001) 'Review,' *Variety*, 9 July, pp 23–4.

Garibotto, V., and Pérez, J. (2016) 'Introduction,' in Garibotto, V., and Pérez, J. (eds) *The Latin American Road Movie*, New York: Palgrave, pp 1–27.

Giddens, A. (1992) *Transformation of Intimacy: Sexuality, Love, and Eroticism in Modern Societies*, Stanford: Stanford University Press.

Godard, J.-L. (1972) *Godard on Godard*, New York: Viking.

Gray, T. (2014) 'Interview,' *Variety*, 28 January, p 61.

Haddu, M. (2005) 'Love on the Run,' *Framework*, 46.2, pp 71–89.

Hirschberg, L. (2003) 'The Way We Live Now,' *New York Times*, 23 March, p 15.

Kael, P. (1966) 'Beauty of Youth,' *New Republic*, 19 November, pp 24–30.

Kaufman, A. (2002) 'Interview,' *IndieWire*, online, 11 March, <www.indiewire.com/2002/03/interview-not-another-teen-movie-alfonso-cuarn-on-truth-style-and-y-tu-mam-tambi-80495/> [accessed December 2018].

Kroll, J. (2007) 'The Cinergetic, Experimental Melodrama,' *Studies in Latin American Popular Culture*, 26, pp 27–46.

Kronke, D. (1995) 'Review,' *Los Angeles Times*, online, 5 June, <http://articles.latimes.com/1995-06-05/entertainment/ca-9660_1_alfonso-cuaron> [accessed December 2018].

Laderman, D. (2002) *Driving Visions: Exploring the Road Movie*, Austin: University of Texas Press.

Lahr-Vivaz, E. (2006) 'Unconsummated Fictions and Virile Voiceovers,' *Revista de Estudios Hispánicos*, 40.1, pp 79–101.

Lang, B. (2016) 'Review,' *Variety*, online, 20 April, <https://variety.com/2016/film/news/alfonso-cuaron-great-expectations-1201757974/> [accessed December 2018].

Lawrenson, E. (2002) 'Interview,' *Sight & Sound*, 12.4, p 19.

Lewis, J. (1992) *The Road to Romance and Ruin: Teen Films and Youth Culture*, New York: Routledge.

Lie, N. (2017) *The Latin American (Counter-) Road Movie and Ambivalent Modernity*, Cham: Palgrave.

López, A. (1990) 'Parody, Underdevelopment, and the New Latin American Cinema,' *Quarterly Review of Film and Video*, 12.1–2, pp 63–71.

Maillat, P. (1965) 'Interview,' *Télé-ciné*, 123, p 23.

Marshall, B. (1988) 'Interview,' *Zappa Wiki Jawaka*, online, 22 October, <http://wiki.killuglyradio.com/wiki/Interview_by_Bob_Marshall> [accessed December 2018].

Menn, D., et al. (1992) 'Interview', *Zappa Wiki Jawaka*, online, <http://wiki.killugly-radio.com/wiki/The_Mother_of_All_Interviews_(Part_1)> [accessed December 2018].

Menne, J. (2007) 'A Mexican *Nouvelle Vague*,' *Cinema Journal*, 47.1, pp 70–92.

'Mexico Finally Revises Film Certification System' (2002) *Screen Daily*, online, 9 April, <www.screendaily.com/mexico-finally-revises-film-certification-system/408835.article> [accessed December 2018].

Mitchell, E. (2001) 'Review,' *New York Times*, 6 October, p A20.

Monsiváis, C. (1995) 'Mythologies,' in Paranguá, P. (ed) *Mexican Cinema*, London: BFI-IMCINE, pp 117–27 (translated by A. López).

Muñoz, J. (1999) *Disidentifications: Queers of Color and the Performance of Politics*, Minneapolis: University of Minnesota Press.

Noble, A. (2005) *Mexican National Cinema*, London: Routledge.

Oropesa, S. (2008) 'Proxemics, Homogenization, and Diversity in Mexico's Road Movies,' *Hispanic Issues Online*, 3.5, pp 95–112.

Pfeil, F. (1995) *White Guys*, London: Verso.

Pulver, A. (2013) 'Review,' *The Guardian*, online, 9 October, <www.theguardian.com/film/2013/oct/09/gravity-alfonso-cuaron-studio-pressure> [accessed December 2018].

Saldaña-Portillo, M. (2005) 'In the Shadow of NAFTA,' *American Quarterly*, 57.3, pp 751–77.

Sandoval, C. (2000) *Methodology of the Oppressed*, Minneapolis: University of Minnesota Press.

Serna, J. (2004) 'El espacio utópico como medio catalizador de la sexualidad masculina y la lucha de clases en *Y tu mamá también*,' *Ciberletras*, online, 11, <www.lehman.cuny.edu/ciberletras/v11/serna.html> [accessed December 2018].

Shary, T. (2002) *Generation Multiplex: The Image of Youth in Contemporary American Cinema*, Austin: University of Texas Press.

Shary, T., and Seibel, A. (2007) 'Introduction,' in Shary, T., and Seibel, A. (eds) *Youth Culture in Global Cinema*, Austin: University of Texas Press, pp 1–6.

Shaw, D. (2007) 'Introduction,' in Shaw, D. (ed) *Contemporary Latin American Cinema: Breaking into the Global*, Lanham: Rowman and Littlefield, pp 1–10.

Shaw, D. (2011) '(Trans)National Images and Cinematic Spaces,' *Iberoamericana*, 11.44, pp 117–31.

Shaw, D. (2013) *The Three Amigos*, Manchester: Manchester University Press.

Smith, P. (2002) 'Heaven's Mouth,' *Sight & Sound*, 12.4, pp 16–19.

Smith, P. (2003) 'Transatlantic Traffic in Recent Mexican Films,' *Journal of Latin American Cultural Studies*, 12.3, pp 389–400.

Sobchack, V. (1992) *The Address of the Eye: A Phenomenology of Film Experience*, Princeton: Princeton University Press.

Sobchack, V. (2004) *Carnal Thoughts: Embodiment and Moving Image Culture*, Berkeley: University of California Press.

Swenson, J. (2011 [1982]) 'Interview,' *Guitar World*, online, 13 August, <www.guitarworld.com/features/frank-zappa-talks-music-money-and-steve-vai-his-first-guitar-world-interview-1982-part-2> [accessed December 2018].

Thanouli, E. (2009) *Post-Classical Cinema: An International Poetics of Film Narration*, London: Wallflower.

Tierney, D. (2018) *New Transnationalisms in Contemporary Latin American Cinema*, Edinburgh: Edinburgh University Press.

Travers, P. (2002) 'Review,' *Rolling Stone*, online, 15 March, <www.rollingstone.com/movies/movie-reviews/y-tu-mama-tambien-251937> [accessed December 2018].

Turan, K. (2002) 'Review,' *Los Angeles Times*, online, 15 March, <www.latimes.com/archives/la-xpm-2002-mar-15-et-turan15-story.html> [accessed December 2018].

Turner, V. (1967) *The Forest of Symbols*, Ithaca: Cornell University Press.

Turner, V. (1969) *The Ritual Process: Structure and Anti-Structure*, Chicago: Aldine.

Udden, J. (2009) 'Child of the Long Take,' *Style*, 43.1, pp 26–44.

Watson, B. (1995) *Frank Zappa*, New York: St. Martin.

Watts, P. (2016) *Roland Barthes' Cinema*, New York: Oxford University Press.

Worrell, M. (2011) 'Sexual Awakenings and the Malignant Fictions of Masculinity in Alfonso Cuarón's *Y Tu Mamá También*,' in Smith, F. (ed) *Sex and the Citizen*, Charlottesville: University of Virginia Press, pp 157–67.

Zappa, F. (1987) *The Guitar World According to Frank Zappa*, Los Angeles: Munchkin.

Žižek, S. (1991) *Looking Awry*, Cambridge: MIT Press.

Žižek, S. (2006a) 'Commentary,' *Children of Men* [DVD region 1], Universal.

Žižek, S. (2006b) *The Parallax View*, Cambridge: MIT Press.

Žižek, S. (2014) 'Commentary,' *Y Tu Mamá También* [DVD], Criterion Collection.

# Index

country club 56–7, 73, 92; figurative 66; social demonstrations 36, 69
puzzle narratives 14, 115
puzzles 4, 27, 30, 39, 104

questioning 1–3, 7, 67, 73, 102, 112; *see also* LGBTQ

reiterations 5, 24, 25, 47, 98–100, 103; glitches 80, 85, 96, 99, 116; stuttered dialogue 88; and travel 75–6, 80, 82; *see also* genre; travel
rhythms 17, 26–7, 48–9, 52, 56, 71; competing 92, 93, 111; songs in counter-rhythm 29, 49, 87, 89
*Risky Business* (1983) 21
rite-of-passage *see* ceremony
road movie *see* genre

sacrifice 34, 41, 51–2, 57–8, 80, 91, 95, 107
Sandoval, Chela 100–2
security *see* insecurity
Seibel, Alexandra 45
sexual arousal: erections 84, 87; foreplay 87, 91; lack of 65, 66; *see also* sexuality
sexuality: fantasy of 1, 54, 56, 59, 68, 71, 73, 87, 93; group sex 20, 56, 72, 103–4; and heteronormativity 13, 39, 45, 67, 71, 84, 93; heterosexual 13, 67, 90; and homoeroticism 84; homosexual 67, 73, 92, 103, 107; and innuendo 53, 84; as intimate exchange 21, 43, 56, 61, 65–6; and objectification 51, 54, 71, 85, 93, 96, 98; and orgasm 57, 61, 66; post-coital 20, 61; and premature ejaculation 61, 88–9, 90, 94; and prostitution 85; queer allegory 19, 103–4; representations of 1–3, 19–20, 59–60, 67, 72, 86, 88–9, 103; seduction 33, 65–6, 87, 89; and sensationalism 32, 72, 91, 93; and sexual identity 60, 67, 73; and sexual revolution 66; and sexual techniques 85, 87, 91, 103; as theme 10, 11, 13, 32; *see also* intimacy; kissing
Shary, Timothy 45, 46, 115–16

Shaw, Deborah 14–15
*Sixteen Candles* (1984) 44–5, 46
Smash Mouth (band) 39
Smith, Paul Julian 60, 63
Sobchack, Vivian 4, 100
social conformity 67, 106–8; and clothing 80, 94; and fundamentalism 2, 116
social demonstrations *see* public-private space
social transgression: and clothing 47, 49; as liberating 115–16; perversity 26, 31, 56; rudeness 19, 27, 53, 60; tantrums 50, 52, 88; vulgarity 42, 49, 64–5, 67, 68
solipsism 3, 52, 57, 61, 81, 88–9, 98; overcoming 69–70, 107
*Sólo con Tu Pareja* (1991) 9, 13, 50
soundtrack dynamism 17, 42, 94, 106–7; compared to Frank Zappa's music 26; emphasizing characterization 52, 55–6, 81–2, 89; emphasizing dialogue 50; emphasizing environment 92
Spanish Conquest 33
Spain, references to 47, 49, 101
spirituality 7, 14, 41, 53, 95; Alfonso Cuarón's 'awakening' 14; and Frank Zappa 26, 27
state sponsorship 9, 75
structuralism 4–7, 22–3, 25–6, 42, 100, 116; and decomposing aesthetics 16, 66–7; graphic collisions 47–9, 57, 61, 68–9, 71, 83, 84, 90, 94, 98–9, 109–10; permutation 73, 88–9, 92, 95, 100; *see also* dialectics
style: and anamorphosis 5, 31, 33, 35–6, 50–1, 55, 59–60, 76; and conceptual continuity 6, 25, 54, 56; and continuity editing 13, 16–17, 22, 25; and establishing shots 62, 68, 87, 92, 106; and long take 13, 16–17, 22, 25; parametric 17, 24–5, 40–1; and shot-countershot 66, 68, 84–5, 88, 95, 107, 113; and split screen 102; and tact 56, 67, 69, 71–2, 75, 83, 92; and xenochrony 75–6; *see also* moving camera; soundtrack dynamism; voice-over

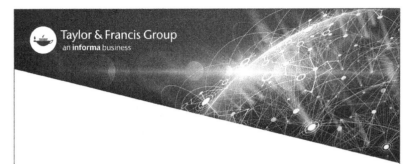

Printed in the United States
by Baker & Taylor Publisher Services